Discover
Britain's
historic
houses

West Country

Discover **Britain's**

Published by Reader's Digest Association Ltd
London • New York • Sydney • Montreal

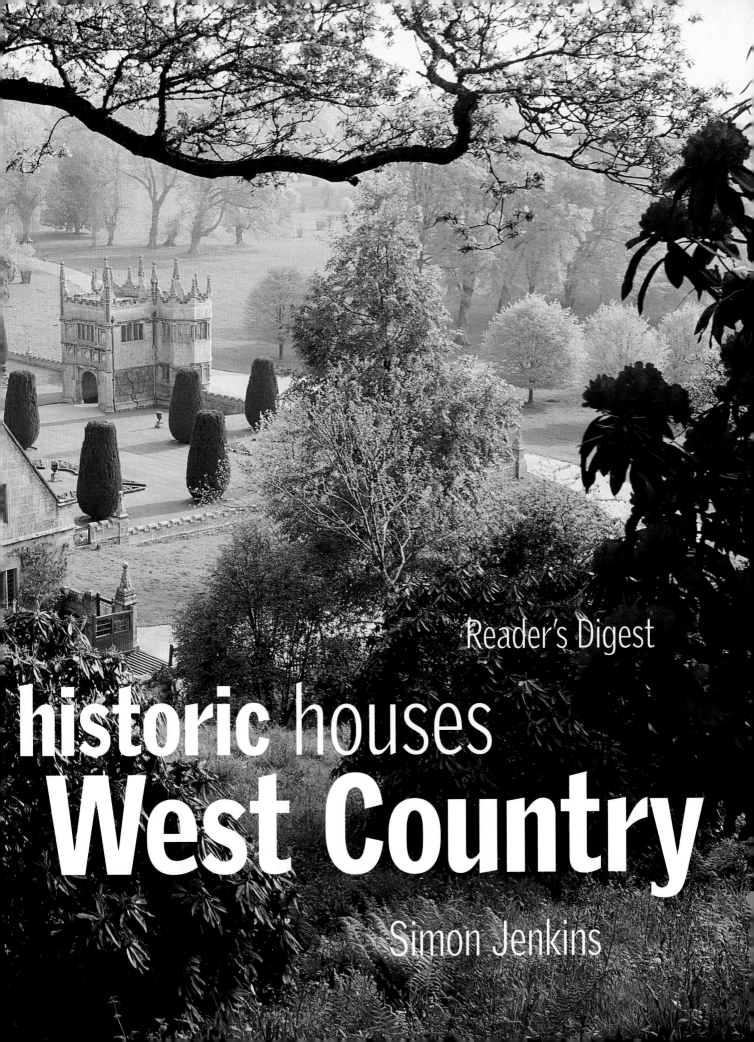

Reader's Digest

historic houses
West Country

Simon Jenkins

Contents

3 SOMERSET

The best in Britain

Castle Howard 102
Charleston 14
Chastleton 56
Chatsworth House 91
Chillingham Castle 111
Chiswick House 36
Claydon House 48
Cothay Manor * 16
Cragside 109
Deene Park 70
Dennis Severs House 38
Dyrham Park 28
Eastnor Castle 53
Eltham Palace 40
Fairfax House 100
Firle Place 13
Forde Abbey 3
Godinton Park 27
Goodwood House 8
Grimsthorpe Castle 78
Haddon Hall 90
Hagley Hall 64
Ham House 35
Hampton Court 34
Hardwick Hall 93
Harewood House 98
Harlaxton Manor 76
Harvington Hall 63

Hatfield House 51
Hever Castle 22
Holkham Hall 80
Home House 37
Houghton Hall 79
Hutton-in-the-Forest 107
Ightham Mote 25
Kedleston Hall 74
Kensington Palace 21
Kingston Lacy 5
Knebworth House 50
Knole 24
Lacock Abbey 29
Lanhydrock * 1
Leeds Castle 26
Levens Hall 104
Longleat 19
Lyme Park 89
Madresfield Court 54
Magdalen College 46
Montacute House * 17
Newby Hall 101
Newstead Abbey 94
Nostell Priory 96
Osborne House 6
Osterley Park 32
Oxburgh Hall 72
Parham House 10
Penshurst Place 23
Petworth House 9
Raby Castle 106
Ragley Hall 55
Restoration House 41

SCOTLAND

Blair Castle 125
Cawdor Castle 129
Craigievar Castle 126
Drumlanrig Castle 112
Duart Castle 122
Dunrobin Castle 130

Dunvegan Castle 128
Edinburgh Castle 116
Eilean Donan Castle 127
Floors Castle 115
Glamis Castle 124
Hopetoun House 118
Inveraray Castle 121
Linlithgow Palace 117
Mellerstain 114
Palace of Holyroodhouse 119
Scone Palace 123
Skara Brae 131
Stirling Castle 120
Traquair House

ORKNEY

ABERDEENSHIRE
Aberdeen

MORAY

HIGHLAND

ANGUS
Dundee

PERTH & KINROSS

FIFE

STIRLING

ARGYLLSHIRE

EAST LOTHIAN
Edinburgh
MID LOTHIAN
WEST LOTHIAN
FALKIRK

LANARKSHIRE
Motherwell
Glasgow

AYRSHIRE

BUTESHIRE

SCOTTISH BORDERS

DUMFRIES AND GALLOWAY

NORTHUMBERLAND
Newcastle upon Tyne
DURHAM
Sunderland

WESTERN ISLES

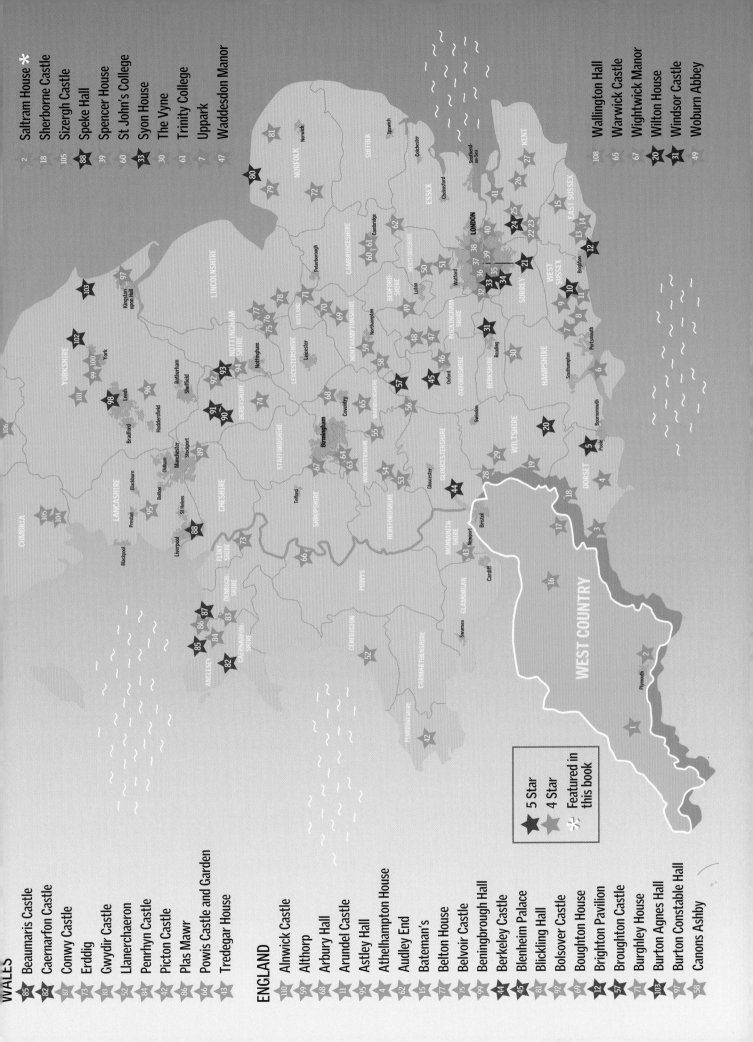

Legend:

★ 5 Star
★ 4 Star
✳ Featured in this book

I visited these buildings after writing a book on English churches and the experience was as moving as it was different. While places of worship were built according to the authority and liturgy of the Church, people built houses for themselves. A house was useful first and beautiful second. From this derives the joy of visiting English houses. They are a conversation between utility and beauty down the ages.

For me this was a voyage of discovery, and in defining the word 'house' I soon found that I could not sensibly distinguish castle from palace, house from hut, roof from ruin. My list embraces any structure in which men and women have laid their heads, provided that they are in some degree accessible to public view. The selection is a personal list and the commentary is a personal vision, warts and all.

Simon Jenkins

Historic houses
of the West Country

The counties of Cornwall, Devon and Somerset are steeped in history, which is visibly reflected in their buildings. This volume celebrates 97 of the most interesting and varied historic homes in the region, from England's oldest surviving domestic structures at Chysauster to the modernist High Cross House at Dartington.

Cornwall feels like a land beyond England: the wild north coast is open to the Atlantic winds, the sheltered bays of the south are almost Mediterranean. The peninsula lay across early trade routes between Ireland, Wales and France. Later, Cornish history was dominated by a few powerful, inter-marrying families – territorial, Catholic and Royalist. Most were rich on tin, but few survived recusancy with their wealth intact.

The building material is mostly granite. The Normans built the castles of Launceston and Restormel and, now much rebuilt, St Michael's

Mount. Henry VIII created what was virtually a western Dover at Pendennis. The county's chief appeal, however, lies in the houses of its historic families: Edgcumbes, St Aubyns, Godolphins, Prideaux, Robartes, Arundells and Carews. Almost all their houses date from the 16th century or earlier. Great Halls hang with ancestral heraldry. Parlours are adorned with portraits galore, many by the 'Cornish Reynolds', John Opie. Great Chambers boast Jacobean plasterwork and tapestries. Furniture is solid oak, with thick, turned legs and muscular arms.

Of Georgian houses, Antony, Pencarrow and Trewithen are outstanding. Jacobean-cum-Victorian Lanhydrock is the National Trust's most visited country house. Outside these houses are their gardens, the glory of Cornwall. The county was a major participant in the exotics craze of the late-19th century, and the imports blossomed in the mild Gulf Stream climate. Rhododendrons, azaleas and camellias burst into collective song each spring.

The **Devon** landscape is much celebrated, from the flanks of Exmoor down the valley of the Exe, with its rich iron-red soil, from severe Dartmoor to the palm trees of Torquay. The county's villages and coastline are as fine as any in England. Devon has two of England's most enjoyable medieval manors, fortified Compton and domestic Bradley, and the great medieval hall at Dartington. Of the Tudor period, there is Cadhay and the great ruins of Berry Pomeroy. As in Cornwall, many Devon families suffered for their recusancy in the 17th and 18th centuries. There are few good houses of this period until the 1770s when John Parker commissioned Robert Adam to decorate Saltram. The Georgian genius for landscape can be seen at Ugbrooke (Capability Brown) and at Endsleigh (Repton).

The Victorians fell in love with Devon. They expanded both Powderham and Hartland in neo-Gothic style. William Burges and J. D. Crace produced a Gothic fantasy for the Heathcoats at Knightshayes. The Singer fortune created the astonishing Oldway mansion at Paignton in Louis XIV style. The 20th century is also excellently represented. Lutyens created Castle Drogo for Julius Drewe. Milne built Coleton Fishacre for D'Oyly Carte. Burgh Island is a rare memorial to English Art Deco.

Somerset brings the great limestone scar of the Cotswolds down across the Mendips to the marshy Levels beyond Glastonbury. It goes on to embrace the Vale of Taunton and the Quantock Hills. Here are some of the southwest's most favoured houses. Somerset is blessed with England's finest stone: creamy near Bath, golden round Ham, deep red across the Vale of Taunton.

The earliest domestic works were modest, as at Muchelney, Cleeve and Martock. They became more substantial as the 16th century progressed. Cothay, Lytes Cary, Clevedon and Gaulden are late-medieval, typical of houses built by merchant owners rich on Tudor prosperity. In Elizabeth's reign houses became even grander, at Barrington and Montacute; Bristol's Red Lodge reflects the great wealth of the city in Elizabethan times.

For the Restoration and Georgian eras there is the spectacular city of Bath, unique in England in the number of town houses open to the public, from the splendour of the Royal Crescent to the modest Herschel House. In the 19th century Salvin restored picturesque Dunster, and vast sums were later lavished by the Gibbs family on Tyntesfield. Edwardian manorialists descended on Barrington, Dillington and, most sensitively, on lovely Cothay. Somerset has looked after its past.

✯ STAR RATINGS AND ACCESSIBILITY ✯✯✯✯

The 'star' ratings are entirely my personal choice (but see note below). They rate the overall quality of the house as presented to the public, and not gardens or other attractions. On balance I scaled down houses, however famous, for not being easily accessible or for being only partly open.

The top rating, five stars, is given to those houses that qualify as 'international' celebrities. Four stars are awarded to houses of outstanding architectural quality and public display. Three-star houses comprise the run of good historic houses, well displayed and worthy of national promotion. Two and one-star houses are of more local interest, are hard to visit, or have just one significant feature.

Accessibility varies greatly, from buildings that are open all year to houses that can only be visited 'by appointment' (rarely, I have broken my rule and included a private property that is not open at all, but is viewable from nearby walks or public gardens). Opening hours tend to alter from year to year, but an indication of how accessible a house is to visitors is given at the start of each entry, together with brief information on location and ownership. Many of the houses are National Trust or English Heritage properties, some are now museums or hotels, others are privately owned by families who open to the public for part of the year (English Heritage grant requirements insist on 28 days minimum). Some owners may, understandably, seek to cluster visitors on particular days. More details for each house are given at the back of this book, and readers are advised to check before visiting.

A final note, houses are, or should be, living things subject to constant change and how we view them is bound to be a subject of debate. I welcome any correction or comment, especially from house owners, sent to me c/o the publisher.

NOTE: On the UK map (pages 6-7) the 4 and 5 star houses in England were selected by Simon Jenkins. Those in Scotland and Wales were selected by the editors of Reader's Digest.

Architectural timeline
and West Country houses in brief

A la Ronde
A sixteen-sided house with conical roof built by two lady Grand Tourists to house their collection of souvenirs. Shell decoration is a particular feature of the interior.

Antony House
An 18th-century mansion, by an unknown architect, begun in 1718. Humphry Repton landscaped the grounds.

Arlington Court
Early 19th century house built by a pupil of the neo-classical architect Sir John Soane. Home to the eclectic and very personal collection of Rosalie Chichester.

Barrington Court
A grand Elizabethan house with a traditional Tudor E-plan exterior. It was restored in the 1920s by architect J.E. Forbes for sugar magnate, Arthur Lyle.

Barrington: Strode House
Built in 1674 as stables for Barrington Court, Strode was converted by J.E. Forbes as a home for the Lyles. It has gardens designed by Gertrude Jekyll.

Bath: 1 Royal Crescent
The first house of the 30 that make up the Georgian Royal Crescent. Begun in 1767 by James Wood the Younger, continuing the development of Bath begun by his father.

Bath: 16 Royal Crescent
One of the central houses in the Royal Crescent, now restored as a hotel. The extensive gardens lead down to Palladian coach houses.

Bath: Crowe Hall
A house built in the 1770s and added to in the 19th century. It was gutted by fire in 1926, but restored in Georgian style in the 1960s.

Bath: Herschel House
The terraced home of astronomers William and Caroline Herschel, furnished with everyday items and examples of early scientific instruments.

Bath: Prior Park
Mansion built by James Wood the Elder for Ralph Allen, a Bath entrepreneur. The house is now a school set in landscaped National Trust gardens that feature a Palladian bridge.

Beckford's Tower
A tower built on the hills north of Bath by William Beckford, inspired by medieval Italian towers. The belvedere on top is crowned with a gold-leaf-covered lantern.

Beckington: Old Manse
A late Elizabethan town house built in stone. The three-gabled frontage dates from around 1620, and the wide entrance hints that it may have been the house of a merchant.

Berry Pomeroy Castle
Ruined Elizabethan house that was converted from a Norman Castle. Substantial parts of the mid-16th-century range remain.

Bickleigh Castle
The medieval gatehouse to what must have been an imposing mansion, destroyed in the 1640s – the current building was created shortly after by adding to the remains.

Boconnoc House
Home of the political Pitt family, which was remodelled by them in the 18th century, with contributions by John Soane. Rescued from decay in recent years by Pitt descendants.

Bodmin Gaol
Bodmin's 19th-century gaol, built of blocks of Cornish granite that resisted attempts at demolition even by dynamite.

Bristol: Blaise House
A late Georgian house with an entranceway designed by Humphry Repton to make the most of views over the Bristol Channel to Wales.

Bristol: The Georgian House
A fine Georgian town house built for a sugar merchant, part of the 18th-century development of the Clifton area of Bristol.

Bristol: Kings Weston House
A grand house by the architect Sir John Vanbrugh, commissioned in 1710 and rescued from potential ruin in 2000.

Bristol: Red Lodge
An Elizabethan town house with oak-panelled rooms. The carved panelling is among the finest to have survived from this period.

Broadclyst: Marker's Cottage
A 15th-century thatched cob cottage with a rare painted wooden partition wall inside. The upper rooms were created during 16th-century modernization.

Broomham Farm
A medieval farmhouse incorporating the original cruck hall with stone and cob walls and a restored thatched roof.

Buckland Abbey
Originally a Cistercian abbey, Buckland was acquired by the Grenville family after the Dissolution and converted into a home. It was later bought by Sir Francis Drake.

Burgh Island
A rare example of an Art Deco residence, designed as a holiday home by architect Matthew Dawson. Now a hotel, it is familiar to many through the novels of Agatha Christie.

Cadhay
A Tudor house with an unusual inner courtyard that features Jacobean statues of the last four Tudor monarchs.

Caerhays Castle
An early 19th-century house built by John Nash in castle style. A Victorian owner filled the gardens with oriental plants.

Castle Drogo
A 20th-century castle designed by Edwin Lutyens and dramatically set in the wild Dartmoor landscape.

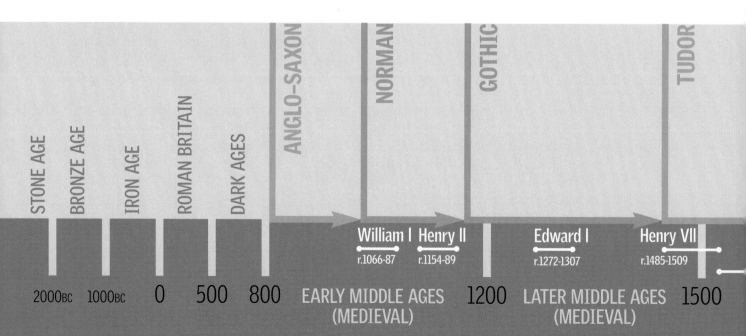

STONE AGE   BRONZE AGE   IRON AGE   ROMAN BRITAIN   DARK AGES   ANGLO-SAXON   NORMAN   GOTHIC   TUDOR

William I r.1066-87   Henry II r.1154-89   Edward I r.1272-1307   Henry VII r.1485-1509

2000BC   1000BC   0   500   800   EARLY MIDDLE AGES (MEDIEVAL)   1200   LATER MIDDLE AGES (MEDIEVAL)   1500

Chysauster: Hut Six
Remains of an Iron-Age village, dating back to around 200BC. Hut Six is one of the most intact dwellings on the site.

Claverton Manor
A Regency mansion built in classical style in 1820 by architect Sir Jeffry Wyatville. The house front features large Regency bow windows, the garden façade is Palladian.

Cleeve Abbey
The remains of a Cistercian monastery, approached through a medieval gatehouse and including the abbot's lodgings, refectory and dormitory.

Clevedon Court
A medieval house, built in around 1320, with an earlier hall and defensive tower at one side and Georgianized interiors.

Clovelly: Fisherman's Cottage
A cottage in former fishing village of Clovelly restored as the residence of a Victorian fisherman, with a loft for drying nets and sails.

Coleton Fishacre
Built in the 1920s as a holiday home for Rupert D'Oyly Carte, this house is Arts and Crafts in style on the outside and Art Deco inside.

Combe House
A Jacobean house, with a Great Hall and 18th-century Rococo plasterwork. Restored in the early 19th century, it is now a hotel.

Compton Castle
A medieval fortified manor house. Abandoned by its owners in the 19th century, it was rescued and sympathetically restored by their descendants in the 20th.

Cotehele
A mainly Tudor house in the Tamar valley, dating from the late 15th century. Tapestries, mostly 17th century, line many of the walls.

Cothay Manor
A late medieval manor house, built in the 1480s and faithfully restored in the 1920s, retaining its medieval character and features.

Cricket St Thomas: Cricket House
A Georgian house (now a hotel) built of Ham stone, with some original interiors by Sir John Soane.

The medieval hall house

Following the Norman Conquest the dominant form of building was the stone keep, but as the Middle Ages progressed and the need for defensible space declined, this was superseded by the hall house or manor house. The main room was the Great Hall, rising to a high wooden roof, probably with a louvre to vent smoke from the central fire and with carved beams reflecting the lord's wealth. The Great Hall was a hospitable place where the family and its dependent community ate together, and where the head of the family conducted the business of the manor. The way of life in these halls turned Norman settler into feudal landlord and lay at the root of English provincial power.

At the formal end of the hall was the dais raised above the earth floor, often canopied and lit by a large side window. Behind the dais were the family's private rooms: a ground floor parlour or undercroft supported an upstairs solar, which gradually extended into a wing at right angles to the hall, sometimes as a Great Chamber. At the other end of the hall a screen kept out the draught from the entrance; above it was often a minstrels' gallery. Beyond the screens passage, a second wing contained kitchens, butteries and servants' quarters.

Given their different uses, the family and service wings were rarely similar in appearance, yet they led to a rough U-shape in early manor houses. As buildings became more elaborate, this developed into the E-plan and H-plan of Tudor and Elizabethan houses – developments that subsumed rather than superseded the Great Hall.

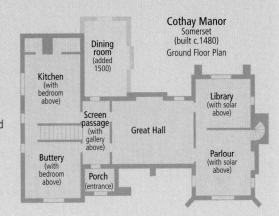

Cothay Manor
Somerset
(built c.1480)
Ground Floor Plan

Cullacott
A group of medieval buildings, comprising a hall, parlour and outbuildings, set around a cobbled courtyard. Inside, some Tudor wall paintings can still be seen.

Dartington Hall
A medieval house dating from the late 14th century, with a rare surviving range of medieval guest lodgings.

Dartington: High Cross House
A Modernist (1932) house designed by William Lescaze for the Dartington Hall Trust as a home for the headmaster of its school.

Dillington House
A mid-1500s E-plan house, converted from an earlier hall house, which was then remodelled in Jacobethan style in the 1830s, giving the house its symmetrical appearance.

Dodington Hall
An intact manor house that includes an Elizabethan Great Hall with minstrels' gallery. An unusual fireplace of 1581 is a fine example of Elizabethan Mannerism.

Dunster Castle
Begun as a Norman stronghold, Dunster has been added to over the centuries with Jacobean and Jacobethan alterations to create the Victorian ideal of a medieval palace.

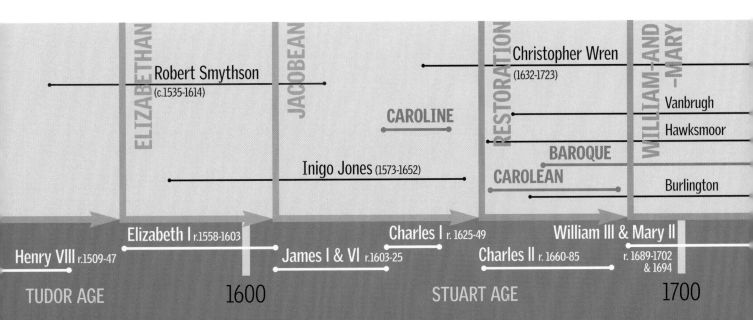

Art Deco

In the years after the First World War the exotic, asymmetric swirls and flowers of Art Nouveau gave way to the zigzags, sunbursts and chevrons of the style that became known as Art Deco. The style appeared before it got its name – from the Exposition International des Arts-Decoratifs et Industriels Modernes, which took place in Paris in 1924-5. Art Deco's geometric shapes and bold colours were in part inspired by the ancient Egyptian artefacts that emerged following the discovery of Tutankhamun's tomb in 1922, but the clean lines and abstract modern look were also a reaction against overstuffed Victorian and Edwardian interiors and the 'old' world associated with the war.

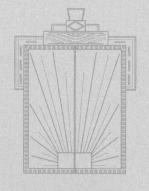

Art Deco resulted in some iconic buildings, most famously New York's Chrysler Building (completed 1930) but also many of London's underground stations and, most familiar to the British public, the Art Deco cinemas that were built up and down the land. In domestic architecture it became associated with the functional modern style of the 1920s and 30s, but it had less impact on external appearance than on interior design – in lighting, door fittings, fireplaces, mirrors and stained glass. From the traditional Arts-and-Crafts exterior of Coleton Fishacre, for example, one would hardly guess at the Art Deco treasure inside.

Endsleigh House
A Regency hunting lodge designed by Sir Jeffry Wyatville and set in a Humphry Repton landscape overlooking the Tamar valley.

Fairfield
A house of many parts – a Georgian façade runs along the side of an Elizabethan E-plan mansion, with the remains of a medieval house to be seen in one wing.

Fursdon House
A medieval family house rebuilt over the centuries, with a Georgian façade added in the 1730s and further additions made in the early 1800s.

Gatcombe Court
A house built on the site of a Roman settlement. The oldest part is 13th century, the exterior mainly 17th century. A Roman well survives.

Gaulden Manor
An early medieval manor dating back to the 12th century. Owners in the 17th century added some extraordinary decorative plasterwork.

Glastonbury: Abbot's Kitchen
Glastonbury abbey was established in the 8th century and rebuilt by the Normans. The stone-built kitchen, dating from the mid-1300s, is a rare survivor of the Dissolution.

Godolphin House
A medieval manor house, improved upon in Tudor and Jacobean times, but then largely neglected until the 1930s. Some parts have since being restored.

Haldon Belvedere
A Gothick-style, castellated, three-sided tower built in 1788 in the Haldon Hills.

Hartland Abbey
A Gothick-style mansion on the site of an old abbey, built in the late 18th century. Additions and new Victorian interiors were provided by Sir Gilbert Scott in the mid 19th century.

Hestercombe House
A Queen Anne house hidden beneath Victorian additions. Above the house lies an 18th-century landscape garden; below is a garden laid out by Lutyens and Gertrude Jekyll.

Killerton House
A Georgian house by the little-known architect John Johnson, set in a park by Robert Veitch. Some rooms are Edwardian, others grandly Georgian.

Kingston House
A mid-18th-century house decorated inside with original Georgian murals and marquetry. The saloon is thought to have been a private chapel.

Kitley House
Remodelled in a neo-Tudor style in the 1820s by G.S. Repton, son of Humphry Repton. Inside, a Georgian staircase dominates the Great Hall.

Knightshayes Court
Begun by William Burges and finished by J.G. Crace, this high-Victorian house is a fine example of the medieval-inspired style then popular in architecture and decor.

Lanhydrock
The original house, dating from the 1620s, was destroyed by fire in 1881 – only the Long Gallery survived. The rebuild created a grand Victorian home in the shell of the Jacobean one.

Launceston Castle
This ruined castle is dominated by a double keep: the outer keep is Norman, the inner keep 13th century.

Lytes Cary Manor
A medieval hall house, built in the 1450s, that was added to and modernized in the 1530s. A Georgian extension sits on one side. It was restored in the early 20th century.

Martock: Treasurer's House
A medieval house built for the local rector, also Treasurer of Wells Cathedral. It contains a Great Hall added in 1293.

Montacute House
A grand late-Elizabethan house built in honey-coloured Ham stone. The west front was built in Elizabethan style in the 1780s, using stone reclaimed from a 16th-century house.

Mount Edgcumbe
The original Elizabethan house was much altered in the 18th and 19th centuries, then this gothicized mansion was destroyed by a WWII bomb. The current house was rebuilt in the surviving exterior.

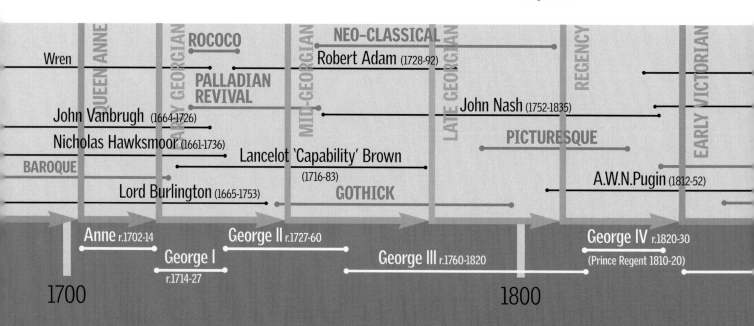

1700

1800

Wren

QUEEN ANNE

EARLY GEORGIAN

ROCOCO

PALLADIAN REVIVAL

MID-GEORGIAN

NEO-CLASSICAL

Robert Adam (1728-92)

LATE GEORGIAN

John Nash (1752-1835)

REGENCY

EARLY VICTORIAN

John Vanbrugh (1664-1726)

Nicholas Hawksmoor (1661-1736)

Lancelot 'Capability' Brown (1716-83)

PICTURESQUE

BAROQUE

Lord Burlington (1665-1753)

GOTHICK

A.W.N.Pugin (1812-52)

Anne r.1702-14

George I r.1714-27

George II r.1727-60

George III r.1760-1820

George IV r.1820-30
(Prince Regent 1810-20)

Muchelney Abbey
A rare example of an intact abbot's lodgings – kitchens, parlours and other living rooms – dating from just before the Dissolution in 1539.

Muchelney: Priest's House
An early 14th-century cottage built to the traditional plan of a hall with a kitchen and an upstairs solar. A fireplace and room above are the only later additions.

Nether Stowey: Coleridge Cottage
The modest home where Coleridge wrote Kubla Khan and other poems. Only the four front rooms are original.

Newton Abbot: Bradley
A medieval manor with fine Gothic details, Tudor wall paintings and 17th-century plasterwork.

Norton St Philip: The George
The stone-built ground floor of this medieval inn supports black-and-white, half-timbered upper floors with oriel windows.

Paignton: Oldway Mansion
A 19th-century mansion, re-modelled in the 20th on the Palace of Versailles. The inside is decorated on a grandiose scale, with a ballroom echoing Versailles' Hall of Mirrors.

Pencarrow
Built in the 1760s, Pencarrow is one of the finest Georgian mansions in Cornwall. The architect was the otherwise unknown Robert Allanson.

Pendennis Castle
A fortress built by Henry VIII in the 1540s to protect the important Falmouth estuary from a threatened French invasion.

Prideaux Place
An Elizabethan house with Georgian and Regency additions, and astonishing plasterwork in the Great Chamber upstairs.

Plymouth: The Elizabethan House
A house dating from about 1580, now preserved as a museum. Three storeys of typical Elizabethan windows rise from the basement.

Plymouth: The Merchant's House
A gabled Elizabethan building; the first and second storeys of the house jut out to overhang the street below.

Plymouth: The Prysten House
A stone medieval house built around a courtyard, probably between 1490 and 1500, for a well-to-do London vintner. The lower floors were for trade, the upper were domestic.

Poltimore House
A Tudor house, modernized in the 18th century to create a stuccoed Georgian mansion. The house is now derelict, awaiting restoration.

Porlock: Dovery Manor
An L-shaped medieval manor house set beneath the slope of a steep hill. A particularly fine hall window faces the street.

Powderham Castle
A fortified manor, added to many times over the centuries; the façade on the courtyard is Victorian neo-medieval. The house overlooks parkland that leads down to the River Exe.

Puslinch
A Queen-Anne style mansion from the 1720s, but with rooms arranged as they would have been in the 1600s with a state bedroom on the ground floor.

Restormel Castle
The circular inner keep of a medieval castle, begun by the Normans and long abandoned.

St Mawes Castle
A fortress built by Henry VIII, facing Pendennis Castle across the estuary, to control the important Falmouth waterway.

St Michael's Mount
A romantic mixture of medieval, 18th-century and Victorian buildings on an island that has signs of settlement dating back to the Iron Age.

Saltram House
Originally a Tudor house, Saltram was altered beyond recognition in the 18th century with with the addition of Palladian façades outside and Robert Adam rooms inside. There is a suite of rooms in Chippendale Chinoiserie.

Sand
An Elizabethan hall house with gabled façade. There is evidence that two hall houses may have existed at the site during the Middle Ages.

Shute Barton
A medieval mansion with gatehouse and courtyard. Inside, on an upper floor, is a Great Hall dating from around 1450.

Stoke-sub-Hamdon: The Priory
A medieval priory farm built in Ham stone, with surviving hall and two-storey solar wing. A large Tudor window and balcony are found in the hall.

Ston Easton
A house built in the 1740s. The central façade is Queen Anne in style, with Palladian flanking wings. The park was by Humphry Repton.

Tapeley Park
A Georgian brick villa with stone porch and decoration, and a colonnaded side elevation. The house is set in sloping landscaped gardens that overlook Bideford Bay.

Tintagel: Old Post Office
A squat 14th-century hall house, built with thick granite walls, a heavy slate roof and stepped chimneys to withstand the Atlantic gales.

Tiverton Castle
Surrounded by medieval outer walls, the courtyard at Tiverton has surviving medieval and Elizabethan ranges as well as an 18th-century villa.

Trerice
An Elizabethan house, finished in 1573, and buit to an E-plan. The exterior has five ornamental gables topped with decorative scrolls.

Trewithen
Built in the late 1730s, this is a simple early Georgian house, rectangular in plan with pavilions on either side.

Tyntesfield
An early 19th-century house remodelled from 1863 onwards in extravagant Victorian gothic style. The interiors have changed little since.

Ugbrooke House
An early castellated house by Robert Adam, begun in 1763. Fragments of Adam interiors can still be seen.

Wells: Bishop's Palace
The picturesque palace of the Bishop of Bath and Wells, surrounded by a wall and moat built in the 14th century. The palace was much altered in the 1840s.

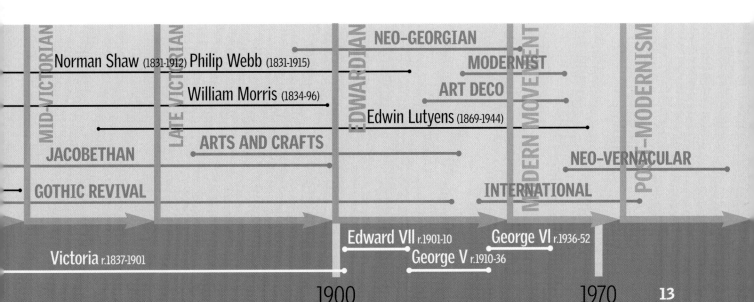

MID-VICTORIAN

Norman Shaw (1831-1912) Philip Webb (1831-1915)

LATE VICTORIAN

William Morris (1834-96)

EDWARDIAN

NEO-GEORGIAN

MODERNIST

ART DECO

Edwin Lutyens (1869-1944)

ARTS AND CRAFTS

MODERN MOVEMENT

NEO-VERNACULAR

JACOBETHAN

POST-MODERNISM

MODERNISM

GOTHIC REVIVAL

INTERNATIONAL

Edward VII r.1901-10

George VI r.1936-52

George V r.1910-36

Victoria r.1837-1901

1900

1970

Corn

St Michael's Mount

wall

Cornwall

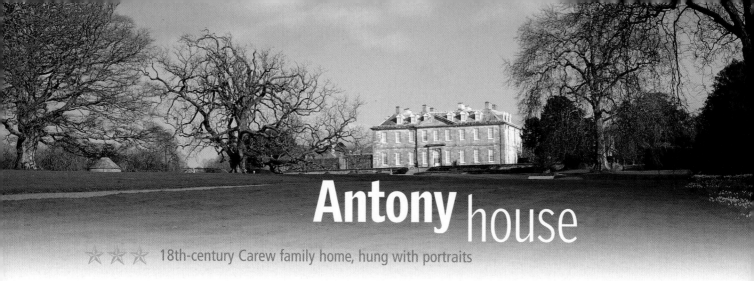

Antony house

2 miles NW of Torpoint; National Trust, open part year

Life was not easy for a Cornish grandee during the Civil War, or for his ladies. Sir Alexander Carew agonized before deciding that he would fight for Cromwell and Parliament, in a county almost universally Royalist. While he was away, the family slashed his portrait in its frame for the shame of it. Then Carew changed sides and decided to fight for the King, and was executed for his treachery. For this glory, the Carew ladies laboriously stitched the picture back together again.

The present Carew house is a rarity in Cornwall, a pure 18th-century mansion of dolls' house prettiness, in silver-grey Pentewan stone. The Carews were one of the oldest and grandest families in the county. Cornwall's most celebrated Elizabethan, Richard Carew, was a lawyer, linguist and poet, remarking with good reason that all Cornish gentlemen were his cousins. It was later, in the reign of Queen Anne, that Sir William Carew married the wealthy Lady Anne Coventry, enabling him to build a new house from scratch. The Carews married Poles and Carew Poles occupy the house to this day, although it is owned by the National Trust.

Begun by an unknown architect in 1718, Antony has a hipped roof, dormers and rusticated quoins. Humphry Repton was paid £30 for a complete Red Book scheme for the grounds. The north front faces a long lawn of three avenues to the River Lynher and Saltash in the distance. The south front welcomes visitors with wings flanking a courtyard.

The interior of Antony is a sequence of 18th-century rooms round an entrance hall and adjacent staircase, once separate but now part of a

Right A grand staircase rises from the entrance hall, richly panelled in stained oak and lit by original early 18th-century glass candle globes. Portraits of Carew ancestors look down from the walls, crowded into every conceivable corner. **Below** This stainless steel cone fountain, designed by William Pye, is made to the same proportions as a large topiary cone of clipped yew found elsewhere in the garden.

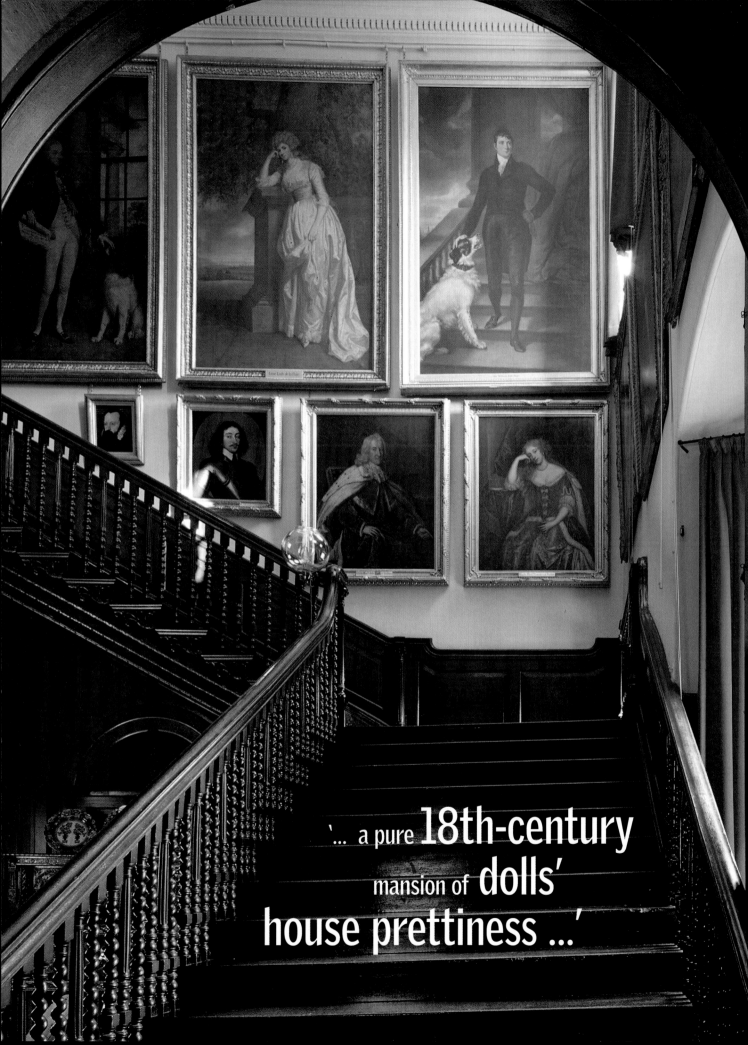

'... a pure 18th-century mansion of dolls' house prettiness ...'

Above left Unsurprisingly, tapestries deck the walls of the Tapestry Room; they show scenes from the life of the Greek philosopher Diogenes. An English giltwood chandelier, from around 1700, hangs from the ceiling.
Above right Among the bedrooms on display at Antony House is one hung entirely with equestrian portraits. Arranged in rows on the wood-panelled walls, the paintings date from the 18th and 19th centuries.

continuous space. So dominant is this space, rising through the heart of the house, that the reception rooms seem almost ante-chambers to it. Dutch oak panelling forms a warm backdrop to regiments of Carew portraits. There are Carews by Gheeraerts, Huysmans, Jonson and Dahl. There is also a late portrait of Charles I, pensive and in black at the time of his trial. It is said to be the only picture showing his beard turned grey.

The staircase is as grand as the hall is intimate, the treads of 'Queen Anne' width but with delicately turned balusters. More Carew portraits climb the walls to the landing, here painted by or 'after' Kneller, Lely, Hudson and Ramsay. The family must be reminded of its longevity and dignity even on its way to bed.

The reception rooms, most of them oak panelled, are crowded with more paintings, including modern works imaginatively commissioned by the present Carews. The saloon has three paintings by Reynolds. One of Pole children playing cricket is on the first floor landing. The girl is seen holding the ball, and the guidebook reminds us that girls allegedly invented overarm bowling to avoid brushing their skirts when bowling underarm. The Small Tapestry Room is filled with happy, rustic pieces from the Soho workshop. The chairs are said to be covered with fabric from papal vestments.

A few bedrooms are displayed upstairs, hung with modern art alongside yet more Carews, Poles, Pole Carews and even Carew Poles. Repton's landscape is visible from most of the rooms. The vista southwards remains spectacular, that northwards glimpses the horrors of modern Saltash. A water sculpture in the garden by William Pye imitates the adjacent topiary of yews.

Boconnoc
house

★ ★ The Pitt family mansion, under restoration

At Boconnoc, 3½ miles E of Lostwithiel; private house, open part year, but groups by appointment all year round

Below This memorial to the Duke of Wellington stands in the park at Boconnoc. Erected on 18th November 1852, the day of the Iron Duke's burial, it is known as the Wellington Clump. At the same time, six trees, each one a different species, were planted around the monument.

Boconnoc is another house of saints. In this case they are Anthony and Elizabeth Fortescue, battling to rescue what was a near-derelict family home. The great house of the Pitt family nestles in the valley of the River Lerryn. In 1969 it was about as desperate as a house can get. Water was pouring through the roof, beams had decayed free of their supports and rot of every sort was rampant. On my visit, a massive enterprise of restoration was in full swing. Not a room was habitable, yet the roof was secure and commitment total. I could only say, good luck.

Boconnoc was a property of the Devon magnates, the Mohuns, until the death of the 4th Baron in a duel in 1712. The old house was then sold to Thomas Pitt, a Madras nabob, for the huge sum of £54,000. He raised the sum

Above The walls of the stairs and landing, and the panelled doors that lead off, feature superb examples of grisaille decoration. Grisaille painting, as the name suggests, is worked in shades of grey or a greyish colour. It was often used to create a *trompe l'oeil* effect and the monochromatic colour scheme was ideal for painting classical subjects so that they took on the appearance of relief sculptures.

by selling the Pitt Diamond to the Regent of France for £135,000. It was later set into Napoleon's sword, a high-risk hiding place. Pitt duly erected the main, rather dull façade. In 1771–2, his grandson, Lord Camelford and a cousin of the prime minister, improved the house and added a grander gallery at right angles overlooking the valley behind.

This Pitt was a figure of some interest. He was a Grand Tourist and amateur architect who built a small house in Twickenham near Walpole's Strawberry Hill and another for himself in Park Lane, Mayfair. In 1778 he met the young John Soane in Italy and became his patron.

In 1786 Soane carried out unspecified repairs at Boconnoc. How much of the present house may be Soane and how much Pitt himself is conjectural. Architect and client were in those days accustomed to working in collaboration. The staircase has extensive grisaille decoration, which may or may not date from this period, but is undeniably grand. The other rooms await attention but I hope a charming children's theatre in a nursery, now occupied by bats, survives.

Overlooking the house is an enclave of church, stables and other outbuildings, already restored. The Fortescues are Pitt descendants. Here is another house lucky in its ancestral owner.

Bodmin gaol

★ The remnants of a major Victorian penal colony

At Bodmin, 6 miles SE of Wadebridge; privately owned, open all year

The cliff of Bodmin Gaol still dominates the town from the north. The prison buildings were sold for demolition in 1929 and most of the roof slates removed. But lime mortar in the joints had fused the granite blocks so strongly that they were resistant even to dynamite. They appear indestructible and have defied all attempts to remove them.

This ranks among the grimmest buildings in England. An early gaol on the site dated from the 1770s. The prison reformer, John Howard, then proposed a new, purpose-built prison in place of the ancient dungeons. The new Bodmin Gaol held 13 prisoners in 1779 and 155 by 1840, from a local population which had less than doubled. Crime waves are nothing new – or at least the zest to imprison is not new. This overcrowding led to pressure for extensions, which were begun in 1855.

They were on a massive scale. The new prison of hard Cornish granite contained 200 cells, a quarter of them for women. This was a complete penal colony. There were hospital cells, laundry, exercise yard, chapel and workrooms. Floors were of slate and cells were cleaned and whitewashed regularly. A treadwheel for milling corn could take up to 32 men.

In 1887, the naval prison in Devonport was transferred to Bodmin, with 105 more cells built on four levels. This was the last Royal Navy prison in Britain, and closed in 1922 six years after the civil prison was shut.

The site was then used as a goods depot, nightclub and is now a bar. Since the gaol shut, the cells have become a tourist attraction and the civilian cells can be visited through the rear of the bar. They have been vividly equipped with tableaux, apparently depicting the crimes for which various inmates were incarcerated. Bodmin makes Madame Tussauds look tame.

The interior of the derelict naval wing can also be seen through barred windows. It stands vast, gaunt and with vegetation growing from its crevices. Mice scamper across the floor. Crows sweep ominously overhead.

As a memorial to the inhumanity of the British penal policy over the ages, Bodmin deserves more extensive access and interpretation.

Caerhays castle

✦ ✦ A 19th-century castle by John Nash, overlooking the sea

At St Michael Caerhays, 9 miles SW of St Austell;
private house and gardens, open part year

Seen from the beach, the castle seems to rise
as if by magic, its battlemented blocks and
towers framed by a bank of trees. It was
designed by John Nash at the height of the
Picturesque movement. The grounds which run
down to Porthluney Cove and Veryan Bay are
awash with exotic plants. The setting is among
the most romantic in Cornwall.

The Trevanions held Caerhays from the
14th century. In 1801 John Trevanion, just
twenty-one and rich on mining royalties, came
into the inheritance and some seven years
later commissioned Nash to rebuild his old
family seat. It was a disastrous decision.
Nash did not come cheap and by 1824
Trevanion was bankrupt and had to flee his
creditors to France. He was not the first man
ruined by an architect.

In 1853, the estate was bought by another
mining family, the Williamses, who own it to
this day. The Victorian J. C. Williams joined
many Cornish landowners in importing
oriental specimens for his gardens. Caerhays
is now a designated home of the national
magnolia collection.

Right, inset Caerhays is one of four gardens that hold
the National Magnolia Collection. Ensuring that the
plants in its care are on display to the public is one of
the responsibilities of a national collection holder.
Species and cultivars, including *Magnolia* 'Caerhays'
shown here, fill the gardens and the collection is being
added to and improved all the time.

'... the castle seems to rise as if **by magic** ... framed by a **bank of trees.**'

The house, which is open in the spring and early summer when the garden is at its best, is a rare survivor of Nash's castellated style. The front hall is Gothick romantic, with an impressive double staircase rising to a landing. In it hangs an Opie self-portrait, a common accoutrement to most Cornish houses. Off the hall are the library and the handsome round drawing room, a dining room and billiard room.

To one side is the 'Museum' with a large painting of a dog. At the time of the Trevanion's impending bankruptcy, the house was visited by the wealthy Angela Burdett Coutts, from whom the family had been hoping for help. Their dog unfortunately bit her footman savagely and she left in high dudgeon. The dog bite was the last straw for the family's fortunes. They duly had it immortalized. A severe fire later in the century destroyed the bulk of the furniture. Most of the contents are 20th century.

Chysauster Hut six

☆ Excavated remains of an Iron-Age village

2½ miles N of Penzance; English Heritage, open part year

Any Chysauster hut will do, but Hut Six is the most impressive. The site is high on the hillside behind Penzance. Its view over West Penwith is superb and the climb worth this alone. Chysauster (pronounced chi-sorster) is England's most exciting Late Iron Age remains – *c*200 BC at its oldest – except that here it was surely 'Tin Age'.

We walk across fields for a quarter-mile from the nearest lane, praying to ancient gods for a clear day. The site must have been chosen so the inhabitants could see trouble coming, notably from the port at St Michael's Mount. If they were involved in the tin trade, they would have been known to have treasure. Others hold they were probably farmers.

The site was first excavated in the 1870s when much damage was done. But we can still make out a settlement of eight houses along a street, reputedly occupied for seven centuries.

Most such ancient villages were of wood and mud. This is of granite, with the pillar stones for the roofs tooled into sockets to receive an upright. It was not a fort, which may have been elsewhere, but a series of oval enclosures about 30ft across. The houses are of a courtyard type. Inside each enclosure are three or four rooms for living and storage. These are built into the surrounding wall, with space for animals in the centre of the yard. Some rooms survive to shoulder height.

Hut Six has the most obvious plan. One of its rooms is raised above the ground, presumably to keep food and family dry. Weather must have been a constant problem, and all the houses have tunnel entrances opening away from the prevailing south-west wind. In the courtyards are runnels for water and evidence has been found of small gardens behind each house.

Cotehele

⭐ ⭐ ⭐ Tudor house, home to a collection of 17th-century tapestries

Near Calstock, 6 miles SW of Tavistock; National Trust, house open part year, gardens open all year

The Georgian Edgcumbes decided they could stand the damp and gloom of Cotehele no longer and made their principal dwelling Mount Edgcumbe (see page 39), down the River Tamar overlooking Plymouth Sound. They left Cotehele alone. It was inhabited by widows, maiden aunts and spinsters. No money was spent and little was altered or rebuilt. The house fell asleep.

Yet the Edgcumbes always appreciated the place. They took Horace Walpole and many others up-river to visit it. By the 19th century, Edgcumbes were even 'adding to' its medieval aura, with tapestries and other refurbishments apparently no longer needed at Mount Edgcumbe. 'Despite the strong air of antiquity,' the guidebook concedes, 'there is little of the Tudor period left in the house and some of the 17th-century pieces were very probably introduced at a later date to enhance Cotehele's romantic appeal.'

The house was given to the National Trust in 1947 and now has a decidedly 'designed' atmosphere, like a French house restored by

Left In the hall at Cotehele, the walls are hung with a collection of arms and armour. The earliest pieces date from the late 1400s although most are from the mid 17th century. **Right** Queen Anne's Room, in the tower, is filled with a bed that is part Tudor, part 17th century. It is hung with 17th-century pale-yellow silk valances and early 18th-century wool damask curtains.

Viollet le Duc. Cotehele's guardians are obsessed with the tapestries, which are superb, but they are neither medieval nor Tudor, almost all dating from the 17th century. Conservationism also admits little natural light, making the house very much a tapestry mausoleum. But these at least re-create the appearance of an old house, a parade of fabric murals depicting everything from Romulus and Remus to Dutch children's games.

Cotehele's pink-grey stone walls lie hidden in a cleft in the Tamar valley. Dating from the late 15th century, it recalls the final flowering of domestic Gothic before the coming of Elizabethan grandiloquence. The principal access was by boat from Plymouth to a private quayside on the Tamar below. The house is arranged round two courts, the formal Hall Court and the lesser Retainers' Court.

The former leads direct to the Great Hall. There is no screens passage and no tie beams or hammerbeams to the high roof. The place is entirely medieval, with heraldic glass in the windows, linking the Edgcumbes to Cotterells, Raleghs, Tremaynes and Carews. The walls are lined with ancient weapons and armour, with the jawbone of a whale and the head of an albatross.

From the Great Hall, the visitor rises to the solar range, with the old dining room, a pretty chapel with a filigree screen and the Punch Room beyond. Here, as elsewhere, tapestries cover every inch of

Above A visitor to Cotehele's old drawing room steps first into a porch, built around the doorway to keep out draughts. It is made up of carved linenfold panels that predate the building of the room in the 1620s. In August 1789, George III and Queen Charlotte visited Cotehele and were given breakfast in this room. During their visit, it is believed that the King and Queen sat on the ebony settee now placed by the window.

the walls. Age has turned the greens to blues, reds to browns and lost the yellows altogether, so one wonders why the National Trust bothers with the ubiquitous blinds.

Many fragments are cut and stitched to fit the rooms, with borders added or removed. Some of the finest needlework is on less prominent furnishings, such as the superb William-and-Mary backing to the settee in the old dining room. Upstairs are the Red Room and South Room, formed from the old Great Chamber, the former with vellum valances to its bed canopy.

Cotehele's tower was added in the 17th century, with three more floors of tapestried rooms. The White Room has Georgian

crewelwork on its bed-hangings. The old drawing room retains a linenfold draught-porch and has a superb walnut cabinet carved with Adam and Eve, *c*1600. The top tower rooms are the loveliest, tiny chambers hung with tapestry fragments and barely enough room for their beds. Charles I supposedly slept in the larger one in September 1644.

Since Cotehele was never built for entertaining or for Victorian comfort, its outbuildings are remarkably simple. The gardens are more recent, terraced down the hillside towards the river. To roam these terraces and lose oneself in the cloistered vegetation is like wandering through the tapestries inside. The interior of this house comes alive outside.

Right Cullacott was once owned by Tavistock Abbey. After the Dissolution, it passed through the hands of several different owners. In Tudor times it was revamped and modernized: a 'retiring' parlour and new bedchamber were added at one end, and the hall was decorated with painted murals – a Tudor coat of arms is still visible high on the wall.

Cullacott

✯ A rare surviving group of medieval buildings set around a yard

4 miles N of Launceston; private house, view by appointment or as holiday let

This is a rare medieval composition of rustic hall, parlour and outbuilding still set round a cobbled yard. It was manorial until the 17th century, when it became a farmworker's cottage, later abandoned. No substantive changes were made in the 18th, 19th or 20th centuries. Only after storm damage in 1989 was the then derelict building recognized for what it was, and its murals revealed. It is rightly listed Grade One. The group is now let as holiday cottages by the neighbouring farm.

The hall is of whitewashed cob on granite footings. It is dated to *c*1480 and open to a low roof. A fireplace was inserted in the early 16th century by new owners, the Blyghte family, and the walls decorated with murals depicting Tudor coats of arms of this period. The windows are original, as is the cross-wall dividing the hall from a tiny upstairs room. In this gallery are murals of St George, suggesting a reasonably prosperous owner.

At the same time, in 1579, a new parlour and upstairs bedroom were built at the upper end of the hall, with smaller rooms projecting at an angle, one for a garderobe. The parlour has a large fireplace and rudimentary plasterwork. The buildings retain original window mullions, flagstones and spiral stairs with irregular 'trip' treads to foil intruders. There is even an heraldic settle.

Above Godolphin has not one but two loggias, open galleries with pillars along one side. One loggia faces out, the other faces an inner courtyard and the ruined range of the Great Hall.

Godolphin house

✦✦ Medieval and Jacobean mansion in process of restoration

5 miles NW of Helston; private house, open part year

Godolphin lies on the side of a hill inland from Mount's Bay. The first house was built by the Godolphin family on the wealth of tin in the 14th century. A more substantial one followed in the 15th, in the conventional Tudor style of two courtyards, a Great Hall, Great Chamber and fine 16th-century stables.

Each generation of Godolphins carried forward the family's fortune and status. By the 1630s, time had clearly come for a more imposing north front. Francis Godolphin rebuilt the entrance front into the main court with an extraordinary double loggia. This is of seven bays of Tuscan columns, one loggia facing out, the other facing in. Such loggias were not unusual in Jacobean or even Elizabethan buildings, but this plan of guests' rooms over a classical cloister was a dashing innovation in Cornwall.

More ambitious plans were not carried out. The Civil War followed, then recession in the tin industry and by the 19th century general decay.

The hall range was demolished, and survives as a ruin across the courtyard. The medieval Great Chamber survives to its east, and is now in process of restoration. Of the first floor rooms, the East Bedchamber has a later Venetian window and 18th-century furnishings. The east range of the courtyard was plainly meant to go with the building of the new loggia range, visible in the present uncomfortable join between the two. Today, it contains a breakfast room panelled in the 18th century and a later hall, with excellent beams and linenfold panelling, which is now the dining room.

The house was acquired by the Schofield family in the 1930s. They have struggled to restore it and recapture its old glory. The stables and outbuildings are completed and work progresses on the main house, although there is as yet little to be seen. The Tudor garden is also being rediscovered. Since the house archives were unfortunately lost in a fire, this is largely a task of archaeology.

Among the interiors at Godolphin saved from further decay is the dining hall. This imposing room is lined with wooden panelling carved to resemble folded fabric, and therefore known as linenfold. The panels around the top of the fireplace are shaped to follow the curve of the opening.

Lanhydrock

⭐ ⭐ ⭐ ⭐ A Victorian mansion within a Jacobean shell

2½ miles S of Bodmin; National Trust, open part year

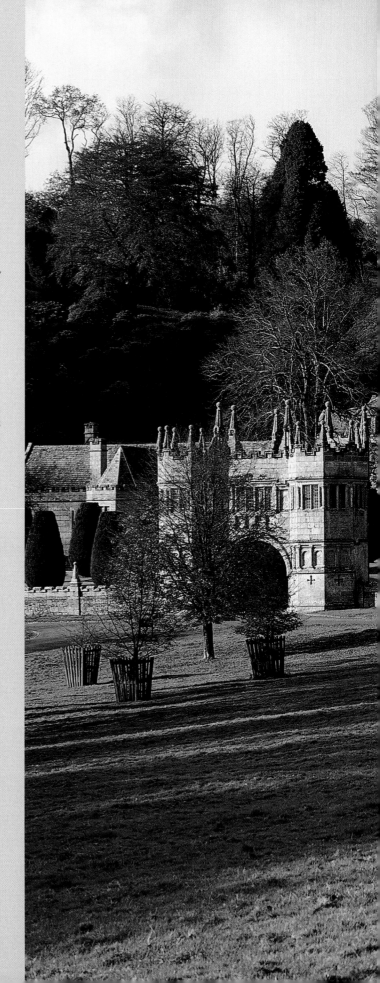

Lanhydrock is always described as being 'lost in a long Victorian afternoon'. But by the time that particular afternoon came round, the former property had seen almost three centuries of them. The original house was begun *c*1620 by Sir Richard Robartes, who spent his tin-mining royalties buying titles from James I. A barony cost him £10,000. His son married the daughter of the Earl of Warwick and became Viscount Bodmin and Earl of Radnor. Such was the wealth of tin.

The family suffered for supporting Parliament in the Civil War, in a county that was staunchly Royalist. After a series of confusing name changes and title revivals, descendants named Agar-Robartes became again Lord Robartes. In April 1881, they suffered the almost total destruction of Lanhydrock by fire. Lady Robartes, a Pole-Carew, died of shock and her husband followed within the year. Undaunted, their son proceeded to re-create a new house within the shell of the old one. Everything except the old Long Gallery which had survived the fire was new, or at least reinstated Jacobean. It was to be a house fit for the age and for the ten Robartes children. The house passed to the National Trust in 1953.

The question for the Trust was whether to treat the house as a restored Jacobean mansion or as a rich Victorian one. The decision rightly went for the latter. The house is one of the best examples in England of a late-Victorian house at work, albeit almost entirely a 1960s creation. The date of the house's reopening, in 1969, coincided with the popular television drama 'Upstairs, Downstairs' and Lanhydrock never looked back. It is the National Trust's most visited house in England.

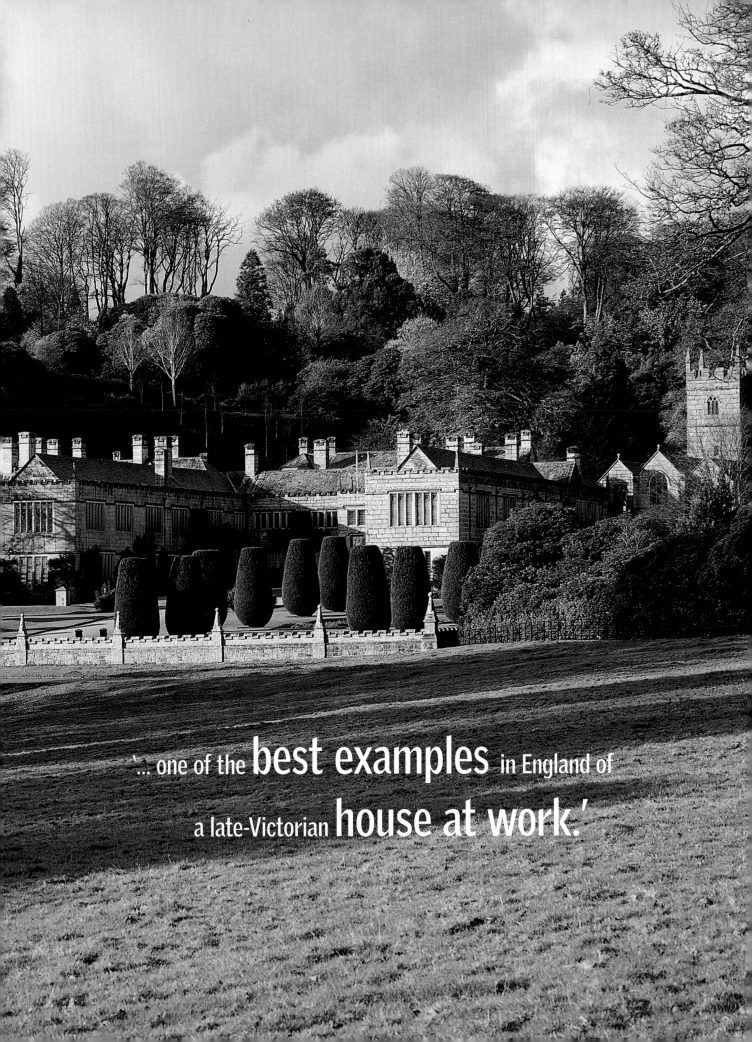

'... one of the **best examples** in England of a late-Victorian **house at work.**'

Right The dairy at Lanhydrock was for the storage of perishable foods. The room needed to be kept cool and so it was built on the north side of the house, with thick tiled walls and a flagstone floor. Runnels of water were piped in from the hills above to help maintain the low temperature.

Below right The Robartes children were looked after by their nanny in a suite of rooms on the first floor. There were day and night nurseries and this separate room set aside for the nanny's use. Known as the nursery scullery, it was furnished with everything that she and the nurserymaids would have needed to carry out their duties.

The house sits in an extensive deer park stretching down to the River Fowey. All its gates and walls survive, as does the 1648 sycamore avenue leading from the gatehouse down to the Bodmin road. The sycamores were doubled with a row of beeches in 1790. In 1990, 1100 trees were lost in a freak storm.

The approach to the house is past the charming gatehouse. This was originally flanked by the walls of an outer quadrangle, yielding the customary Elizabethan inner and outer courtyards. Today an avenue of yews leads from the gatehouse to the present entrance forming a dramatic, essentially Victorian, composition. The interior is a warren of rooms, 50 of them open to the public. It was designed by Lord Robartes for Victorian entertaining in style, a labour-intensive activity. He ordered a new south-east wing round spacious kitchens, with male and female indoor staff carefully segregated. Men and women were to work without meeting each other, or meeting members of the family. The butler's and housekeeper's quarters are also apart. Attic bedrooms for each sex were reached by separate stairs. A prayer room was also set aside for their daily worship. The intention was 'to make them more moral and more efficient'.

Even the children and their nannies had a wing (and staircase) to themselves. There was also a separate staircase so male guests could go to bed after billiards or smoking without disturbing the rooms allocated to ladies. Even His Lordship's Bedroom with its Pugin wallpaper is in a separate suite from

Above The large kitchen at Lanhydrock is furnished with a long table and equally massive dressers, piled with pots, pans and plates. In the house's heyday, the table would have been surrounded by servants preparing meals, all working at different tasks under the watchful eye of the cook. Finished dishes were passed through the hatch at the far corner of the room (centre of picture) and taken to the servery, then from there to the dining room.

Her Ladyship's, although they could meet through sharing a common bathroom.

A visit to Lanhydrock is a voyage through these antique arrangements. The hall, its granite fireplace a survivor from the old house, is decorated as for Christmas. The dining room with Morris wallpaper is laid ready for dinner. The table centrepiece is a spectacular sculpture of a camel and palm tree, in pure tin from the grateful miners of Redruth. The kitchen wing displays farm eggs ready to be sent by train to the house in London, where the family would eat only produce from their own estate.

The south wing comprised the smoking room and billiard room, heavy with stuffed trophies of deer, fox and moose. School photographs adorn the walls. In the adjacent steward's room stands a rabbit gun and Gladstone bag. Above is Captain Tommy's Bedroom, dedicated to the Robartes son and heir, killed at the Battle of Loos in 1915. Everything contained in his field kitbag is displayed, including rouge which he used to conceal any facial pallor of fear from the men under his command. His death devastated the family. The room was locked by his sisters and left as a shrine to his memory. Beyond is the nursery range, a row of beds arranged like a school dormitory. The table carries much politically incorrect literature about gollywogs and foxhunting.

At every turn, one is plunged behind green baize doors to see how the house 'worked'. There are rooms full of linen, travelling trunks, bedpans and pots, trolleys and dumb waiters. Cigarettes remain in servants' ashtrays. Loofahs rest on bathtubs. All this is not Edwardian survival, it should be said, but National Trust creation on the basis of research into how such a house might have been.

The reception rooms come almost as a relief from this domesticity. The drawing room over the hall is furnished in 18th-century style, hung with family portraits by or after Reynolds, Dahl and Kneller. Beyond is Lanhydrock's one grand

Above The heavily panelled smoking room was a male preserve, furnished with deep-buttoned armchairs and hung with sporting trophies. **Below right** The dining room table is set as it might have been for dinner at the end of the 19th century. The fruit-topped centrepiece is made of tin and was given to the Robartes by local tin-miners as thanks for the infirmary they established at Redruth.

room, the old Long Gallery. It was saved during the fire by the neighbouring range being dynamited during the fire. The walls are panelled and hung with portraits, but all attention focuses on the barrel vault. The plasterwork is similar to that at Prideaux Place, depicting scenes from the Old Testament, surrounded by animals and birds. Executed by the ubiquitous West Country decorators, the Abbot family of Bideford, probably in the 1630s, it harks refreshingly to an era before the formality of the rest of the house.

Above The Gallery at Lanhydrock was miraculously saved from the fire in 1881, thus ensuring the survival of the early 17th-century plasterwork ceiling. This is decorated with scenes from the Old Testament. Along the south side of the ceiling are the stories of Adam and Eve, Cain and Able, Noah, and Abraham and Isaac; the life of Jacob is depicted along the north side.

Launceston castle

★ Fortress with impressive double keep

At Launceston, 8 miles NW of Tavistock; English Heritage, open part year

There are few signs of domestic comfort left at Launceston Castle. The fortress continues to dominate the town and its surrounding valley. The motte and bailey were erected by the Normans to control the country between Bodmin and Dartmoor at the border bridge over the River Kensey. This was the seat of the Earls of Cornwall, customarily brothers of the monarch. The castle was extended by Richard of Cornwall in the 13th century but declined at the end of that century when Duchy administration was moved to Lostwithiel. Assize courts remained and the castle became a dreadful prison; demolished in favour of Bodmin (see page 21) in 1842, it fell into disuse.

What remains is a fine gateway in the wall facing the town and, within, a sensational double keep crowning a high mound or motte. The remains of the bailey, including the site of the Great Hall, are in the park. All attention is focused on the keep. This is now an outer wall or Norman shell keep within which is a later high tower inserted in the 13th century. Although a massive pile of ruined masonry, it retains stairs and two habitable rooms, one with a fireplace.

This must have been a bleak posting. The keep was later used as the gaol. From the top of the castle flutters the English Heritage flag. Surely the standard of the Duchy of Cornwall would be more appropriate.

'This must have been a bleak posting.'

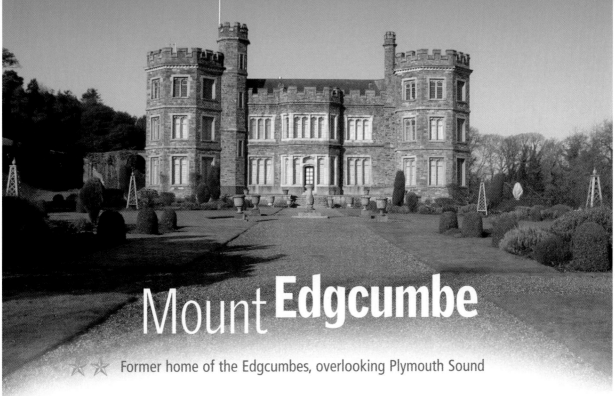

Mount **Edgcumbe**

★ ★ Former home of the Edgcumbes, overlooking Plymouth Sound

3 miles SE of Torpoint; museum and gardens, open part year

The seat of the Edgcumbe family since the 16th century is no longer its old self. This ancient Cornish family survived all centuries until the 20th. Then, like so many families, it watched war, social upheaval and taxation drain it of the resources and the will to continue. The house is now owned jointly by the City and County of Plymouth and Cornwall, and the peninsular landscape is an ornamental park. This park, with its national collection of camellias, is nothing short of sensational in spring – like a sustained explosion of botanical fireworks overlooking Plymouth Sound.

Sir Richard Edgcumbe built the house in the 1550s to supplement his other home up the River Tamar at Cotehele (see page 26). The house was on an unusual plan for the early-Elizabethan period. Four round towers framed symmetrical façades, with reception rooms enclosing a Great Hall in the middle. The nearest parallel is Wollaton (Nottinghamshire), but that was not built until 1588. Sir Richard appears to have wanted a blast of ostentation to overlook the Royal Navy's western base.

This house is no more. It was classicized then gothicized in the 18th and 19th centuries. The towers were made octagons and the Great Hall became a two-storey classical temple. Porch and conservatories were added. Then all this vanished when a bomb, presumably aimed at Plymouth, hit the house in the Second World War. The 6th Earl of Mount Edgcumbe, though seventy-nine and with his only son and heir killed in action, determined to rebuild it.

With Adrian Scott as architect, he created a 1960s mansion inside the shell of the old house. The exterior survives as a russet sandstone mansion in the Elizabethan style of the original, with stone mullioned windows and battlemented roof. The family resumed occupation in 1964 but within a year the Earl had died and the estate was inherited by one New Zealand relative and then another, both returning dutifully to live in Cornwall. The last moved out in 1987 and house and grounds were sold jointly to the relevant local councils.

The interior is now very much a museum, furnished in what the guide calls 'a generalized 18th-century style'. Among the exhibits are seascapes by van der Velde and family portraits, including one by Reynolds. A picture of the staff of Mount Edgcumbe at the turn of the 20th century shows 172 people, including 14 'pensioners'. It would have been much the same four centuries earlier. Such is the change a century has wrought.

Pencarrow

★★★ Georgian house, with pictures by Reynolds among its treasures

4 miles NW of Bodmin; private house and gardens, open part year

The house dances attendance on its family and garden. The family is that of the Molesworth-St Aubyns, whose tree since the 16th century is a spider's web of Cornish gentry. It could at one point march on 'family' land across much of the West Country. An ancestor in the 13th century accompanied Edward I to the Holy Land. The current Molesworth-St Aubyn Bt is the 16th. A collateral line inherited St Michael's Mount (see page 49).

Pencarrow garden, at least in April, is a stupendous display of rhododendrons, azaleas and, later, hydrangeas. The drive is like a botanical guard of honour and the house sits in a bowl of exotic flowers and trees, muting its severe classical frame. It was built in the 1760s by a young Yorkshire architect, Robert Allanson, otherwise unknown. In the 19th century, the

interior received fittings from the family's seat at Tetcott in north-west Devon. The sumptuousness of the panelling matches anything in the West Country. Indeed, from its graceful Georgian exterior to its lush interiors, Pencarrow ranks with Antony House (see page 16) as a rare example of Cornish 18th-century opulence.

The entrance doubles as a library. The room is panelled in pine, with fitted bookcases below family portraits. On show is a set of intriguing Victorian glass pens. Next door is an exquisite music room. Its furnishings imported from Tetcott include a classical alcove once filled with an organ but now containing a statue of a Grace. The room's panel decoration, ceiling plaster and even the picture frame over the fireplace are in Rococo style. Two Oswald Birley portraits depict the present owner's

great-grandparents, but twenty-seven years apart. Thus the husband is a dashing young man, his wife a grey-haired elderly woman, a charming and unusual contrast.

Chairs in the drawing room are upholstered with damask, claimed, like many in Cornwall, to have been taken from a captured Spanish galleon. The inner hall, splendidly arched, contains a curious stove whose flue goes underground. It is surrounded by a large collection of dolls and pushchairs. Pencarrow is stuffed with teddy bears. In the dining room is a great rarity, a complete set of Reynolds portraits painted at one time and of one family, the men confident, the women wistful.

The upstairs bedrooms are as rich as the reception rooms. Actresses (or their producers) who have made films in the house have been persuaded to leave dresses for exhibition, left casually as if just disrobed. The final ante-room contains Pencarrow's two treasures. Devis's group portrait of the four Misses St Aubyn is among his masterpieces, and it is delightful to find it on this Cornish wall rather than languishing in a museum. Before it sits the Pencarrow Bowl. This was made in China for the English market, and depicts an English foxhunting scene. The Chinese considered it bad luck to depict a fox being killed, so the animal in the centre looks distinctly like an otter.

Pendennis castle

★ A Tudor fortress built to guard the mouth of the Falmouth estuary

At Falmouth, 6 miles S of Truro;
English Heritage, open all year

The estuary of the River Fal, known as Carrick Roads, was the 'Key to Cornwall', the finest harbour west of Plymouth and natural objective of any invading fleet. Henry VIII fortified it in the 1540s against the French, leasing the land from the local Killigrew family, who became hereditary captains of the castle.

During the Civil War, Pendennis was held for the king by the Arundells of Trerice. Both Charles I's wife, Henrietta Maria, and their son, the future Charles II, escaped England through its gates, the queen being described as 'the most worne, weak pitifull creature in the world'. The castle then defied a five-month Parliamentarian siege from both land and sea in 1646, being surrendered to Fairfax with its colours flying.

The site is as starkly exposed today as it was then. The climb from Falmouth reaches a deep moat, a gatehouse, wall and then bare lawn with no apparent boundary but the sky and sea. Victorian and Edwardian barracks fill one side, the Tudor fortress the other. The latter is reached by a bridge into the central keep. Apart from one Georgian window, this retains the slit openings and battlements of the original fort.

Inside the fort is the governor's residence which lasted into the 18th century. The rooms were panelled for warmth and have been restored with table, chairs and even a four-poster bed. A place of war is turned into what might be a country rectory, demure china on the table and Dutch tiles on the wall. The lower gun room has thick bastions and narrow openings for guns. The upper gun room has been filled with canons, ropes, waxworks and tape recordings of explosions.

A spiral staircase leads to the roof turret, the point from which the Armada was first sighted from English soil. The vista stretches from the Lizard to Plymouth. Beneath the main fort are subsidiary defences, showing Pendennis pressed into service throughout history. It is the Dover of the west. The outer bastion was last converted as a look-out during the Second World War and contains an exhibition of its defences during that period.

The Spanish Armada

The Spanish Armada was first sighted off the Lizard from Pendennis on 29th July, 1588. In the days that followed, English ships harried the Spanish all the way up the Channel, but even a fireship attack at Calais and a battle off Gravelines failed to sink a single ship. It kept the Spanish so busy, however, a landing was unthinkable. Eventually a heaven-sent gale scattered the Armada in the North Sea and the Spanish were forced to make their way home round Scotland and Ireland; of the 138 ships that left Spain, only 67 returned.

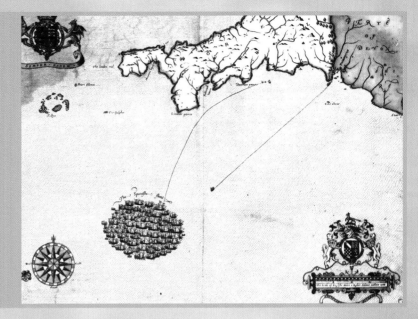

The main keep of Pendennis – seen here from gun mountings on the outer bastion – dominates the site. Its peninsular position and circular plan made the castle the ideal vantage point from which to guard the Cornish coast. From the turret, the view stretches from the Lizard in the west to Plymouth in the east. **Top left** The castle's governor lived in reasonable comfort in his own quarters, adjacent to the keep on the inland side of the fortress.

Prideaux place

★★★ An Elizabethan house with Georgian and Regency Gothick additions

At Padstow, 5 miles W of Wadebridge; private house, open part year

The Prideaux family has always backed the wrong side. Or almost always. They came over with the Conqueror and after the Dissolution acquired land on this sublime site in north Cornwall. The house sits in splendour on a hill overlooking Padstow and the sea, and is Elizabethan, Georgian and Regency Gothick in equal measure. The Elizabethan front of what was then called just Place (for palace) was built in 1592. This façade is mostly as built, warmly clad in creeper above a terrace. The remainder of the exterior was gothicized in 1810, on the garden front with full Gothick embellishments.

The porch leads into a screens passage and the Great Hall, now the dining room. This is entirely panelled in oak and has an original Great Chamber above it. The screen, probably imported in the 19th century, is no ordinary piece. Filled with superb marquetry, its panels are crowded with foliage and animals. The fireplace is flanked by a carving of Elizabeth I standing on a pig, symbol of vice. The whole composition is robust and yeoman-like.

Beyond is the family's morning room, with numerous Opies of the Prideaux-Brunes, still the present owners of the house. Here is also an 18th-century pastel of a Prideaux by the Italian portraitist, Rosalba Carriera. She allegedly fell in love with the sitter while drawing him, and wrote him a letter to that effect which she slipped into the frame, asking for his devotion in return. The letter sadly

remained hidden in the frame until the picture was cleaned in 1914.

The drawing room steps abruptly forward to 1810 and Prideaux's remodelling in the Gothick style. The room contains two exotic Rococo mirrors and looks out through the bay window onto the south lawn. Next is the Grenville Room, acquired and installed complete from another Cornish house, Stowe at Kilkhampton, in the 1720s.

The wall carvings are in the style of Grinling Gibbons and are sumptuous. Three panels by Verrio appear to have come with the room, which has been restored with green panelling and gilded picture frames.

The remarkable Gothick ceiling to the staircase is by an unknown hand, balanced by niches, iron balusters and Gothick window tracery. Upstairs is Prideaux's pride and joy, the Great Chamber over the hall. The astonishing

Above In the Great Hall, the fireplace features this unusual carving of a woman standing on a pig. The pig is meant to be a symbol of vice, the woman is believed to be a representation of Queen Elizabeth I. **Left** Above the Hall lies the Great Chamber. The magnificent plasterwork ceiling had been hidden from view since the late 18th century and was only revealed again in the 1980s.

ceiling was hidden behind another ceiling until discovered by the present owner as a small boy, when crawling across the rafters. It is a companion to the Jacobean ceiling that survived the fire at Lanhydrock and is clearly by the same hand, supposedly the Abbot family near Bideford. Scenes depict stories from the Old Testament and comprise a biblical and morality tale in one. It is possible these are themes that Catholic Cornishmen may have felt unable to display in their Reformation churches.

A divide in the stairs leads to the library, which is once again in Gothick style. The walls are green and the ceiling blue. Indeed the whole house is an exercise in the deployment of bold colour, and much the better for it. In the library is a portrait of the present owner, Peter Prideaux-Brune, in his barrister's robes, with his teddy bear mascot by his side. Prideaux specialises in cross-Channel visitors, welcomed in fluent French, echoing its Norman forebears.

Restormel castle

⭐⭐ The circular inner keep of a medieval castle

1 mile N of Lostwithiel; English Heritage, open part year

Edward III knew the Cornish would be trouble and ruled it through his son and heir, the Black Prince, Duke of Cornwall. Its strongholds are held by the Prince of Wales, as Duke of Cornwall, to this day.

Restormel previously belonged to the Earls of Cornwall. It was begun by the Normans and achieved its present dramatic form in the 13th century when neighbouring Lostwithiel became the base of Crown administration in Cornwall in place of Launceston. It degenerated from the 14th century onwards, a neglect that preserved its remarkably unaltered circular form.

The castle was derelict by 1610 when the historian Norden reported that 'the whole castle beginneth to mourne and to wringe out harde stones for teares'. This was an unusually evocative conservationist sentiment for that era.

Restormel Castle has a remarkable presence above the valley of the River Fowey. Apart from devastatingly intrusive modern power pylons, the view from its walls is sylvan. Shall we ever be rid of the pylons? The outer bailey and curtain wall have gone, but the inner keep with its dry ditch is remarkably intact. The crenellated wall can be walked uninterrupted. This is one of my favourite English castles.

The inner keep is technically a shell castle. The circular plan is of a palisade forming the outer wall of buildings arranged round a small inner court. Each chamber, hall, kitchen and chapel occupies a sector of this internal plan.

Only the kitchen walls stand to their original height, but all rooms are discernible. The most important are raised above extensive ground-floor storerooms. Restormel is an eerie, private place, lost with its memories. It is more evocative of the past than the scrubbed fortresses of the coast. Perhaps this is one where the authorities could allow the return of some creeper.

'Restormel is an eerie, private place, lost with its memories.'

St Mawes castle

At St Mawes, 6 miles S of Truro; English Heritage, open all year

St Mawes was the lesser of the two Fal fortresses, and gazes westwards across the estuary to its big brother, Pendennis Castle. It overlooks the pretty resort from which it takes its name and looks as unmilitary and inoffensive as the villas that line the coast above it. Like the forts that Henry VIII built along the coast of Kent and Sussex, St Mawes is essentially a firing platform to defend the harbour, formed of a clover leaf of bastions.

These castles were also an assertion of the King's sovereignty in Cornwall, hence the bold coat of arms over the gateway, with the inscription in Latin, 'Henry thy honour and praises will remain for ever'. Other mottos in praise of the king are found elsewhere in the castle. Only the most rudimentary attempt was made to defend the castle from those who might disagree. On the landward side are battlements, a ditch and gunloops.

The castle interior is divided between the domestic chambers of the governor and the gun rooms and batteries. All are well preserved and much polished by English Heritage. The central tower is of three floors, with three rooms divided by partitions and with fireplaces in all of them. Above is the barracks room and below a kitchen with a large fireplace. The roof offers a fine view over Falmouth Bay.

Below the castle on the shore is another range of positions for the mounting of artillery. This Shore Battery displays an assortment of canons from different periods of military defence.

St Michael's mount

★ ★ ★   Ancient monastery and castle set on an offshore island

Near Marazion, 3 miles E of Penzance; National Trust, open all year (winter openings depend on favourable tides and weather)

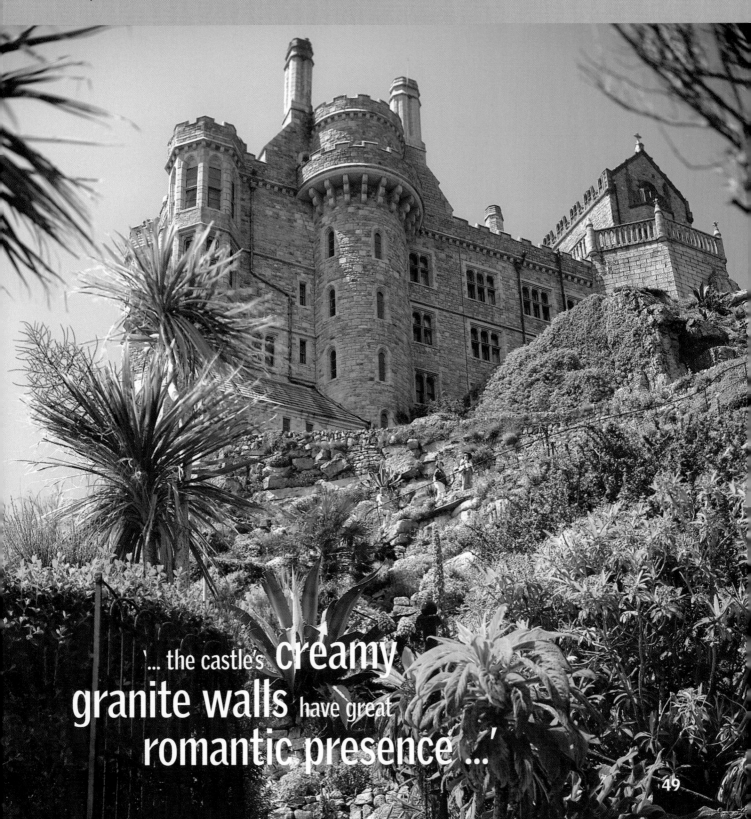

'... the castle's creamy granite walls have great romantic presence ...'

An offshore island, a monastery and a castle must attract mystery. St Michael's Mount sits picturesque in Mount's Bay. The causeway linking it to the mainland remains open only at low tide and on my first visit many years ago, an amphibious vehicle had to convey me to the site. Although much altered in the 18th and 19th centuries, the castle's creamy granite walls have great romantic presence, rising today above the island's sub-tropical gardens and the pretty harbour village below.

The Mount had been a natural refuge and centre for trade since prehistoric times, probably the ancient port of Ictis. Iron Age traces have been found on the slopes, presumably of early traders shipping tin, crossing Cornwall from the north coast and from Wales and Ireland beyond.

The rock and its church were long dedicated to St Michael, fighter of the Devil and thus blessed with churches on rocks and high places. In 1135 the Benedictine monks of Mont St Michel in Normandy were invited to establish a priory in Cornwall. Their church was destroyed by an earthquake in 1275 and never rebuilt with the splendour of its French parent. The surviving small priory was suppressed by Henry V as alien and granted to Syon Abbey by Henry VI in 1424.

The Mount was favoured as a stronghold during the Wars of the Roses and was used as a base by Perkin Warbeck during his brief rebellion against Henry VII. After the Dissolution, it was occupied by military governors and held for the King during the Civil War. With its surrender to Parliament in 1646, the captaincy passed to Colonel John St Aubyn, who later bought the Mount and adapted it as a residence in 1659. His family occupies the East Wing of the castle to this day, albeit since 1954 as leaseholders of the National Trust.

A visit to the Mount is primarily a scenic experience. The building is an amalgam of medieval, 18th-century and Victorian work. The medieval parts are the gatehouse and hall, church, Lady Chapel and refectory, with garrison quarters underneath. The church is of the 13th century, while the monastic refectory survives as the Chevy Chase Room. This was the Tudor Great Hall and retains a magnificent arch-braced roof. It takes its name from the plaster reliefs that line its walls, depicting hunting scenes. Down the middle of the room is a massive Jacobean oak table, flanked by monastic chairs, one of them medieval from Glastonbury.

'An offshore island, a monastery and a castle must attract mystery.'

Above The son of Colonel John St Aubyn, who bought the Mount in 1659, was made a baronet by Charles II. It was the third baronet of that name who planned the conversion of the ruined Lady Chapel into two drawing rooms. He died in 1744, probably before the work on the rooms was completed.

The surprise of St Michael's Mount is the Georgian conversion of the old monastic Lady Chapel. This stands detached on a platform overlooking the sea. The interior is in florid Strawberry Hill Gothick of *c*1750, in pale blue with white ogival arches, an ornamental ceiling and pretty oriental pediment to the overmantel. The room, in effect two rooms divided by a fireplace with chinoiserie pediment, is strongly reminiscent of Shobdon church in Herefordshire. The smaller room contains a rare landscape of the Mount, by the Cornish portraitist, John Opie. He was extravagantly acclaimed by Reynolds as 'Caravaggio and Velasquez in one'.

The rest of the castle displays the old barracks and museum rooms. Thanks to the National Trust and the St Aubyn family, the island and its little port have been well conserved, a far cry from the insensitive tourist development round most of Penzance.

Tintagel Old post office

★★ A medieval hall house built of granite and Cornish slate

At Tintagel, 10 miles N of Wadebridge; National Trust, open part year

Forget King Arthur and the Round Table. The soggier side of the Victorian imagination pervades Tintagel as it does Glastonbury. There is no evidence that anyone called King Arthur came near the place. The dramatic ruins on an offshore rock are medieval. More real by far is the Old Post Office, a beguiling stone hall house dating from the 14th century.

The National Trust owns the house and has appropriated one of the precious medieval rooms as a shop as well as a reinstated post office. The building crouches low and heavily buttressed on the main street, so low as if about to slink away from tourists battering on its door.

The house sags under the weight of its slate roof which, above the granite of its walls, seems to have emerged fully formed from the ground beneath. The central chimney tapers in three steps to the top to reduce resistance to the Atlantic gales. This is a house that does not intend to be blown away.

The plan is of a medieval hall and parlour. The entrance is into a passage, with the hall open to the roof on the left. The parlour has an original slit window deep in the wall. A small spiral stair leads up to a bedroom, recently furnished in Victorian style.

A gallery, probably another bedroom, overlooks the hall. Huge roof beams support the heavy Cornish slates overhead. A fire normally burns in the big fireplace below, agreeably filling the house with wood smoke. Above it is a shelf with two candles and an early gun.

Trerice

⭐⭐⭐ An Elizabethan house with scrolled gables

3 miles SE of Newquay; National Trust, open part year

Trerice, pronounced tre-rice, is a hidden Elizabethan house concealed in the hills behind Newquay. The house was finished in 1573 for Sir John Arundell and has been little altered since. The Trerice estate passed through various hands, including the Aclands in the 19th century, and went to the National Trust in 1953.

Unlike the earlier Elizabethan house of Cotehele, the façade of Trerice makes some effort at outward symmetry and display. It is an E-plan house with five wayward ornamental gables framing its attic windows, of Cornish limestone that changes colour with the light, from yellow to pink to grey. The scrolls on these gables were said to be unique at the time, comparable only to gables in the Low Countries, where Arundell had been a soldier. Two of the gables were restored in the 1950s after part of the house was thought about to collapse.

The interior remains Elizabethan. The entrance under the porch is into a screens passage to the Great Hall, with the family chambers to the south.

The hall is a fine room, its ceiling of geometrical plasterwork with large pendants. Trerice's plasterwork was celebrated and much imitated elsewhere in Cornwall. The overmantel is dated 1572, its fanciful scrollwork a foretaste of Rococo. The hall is well stocked with 17th-century chairs, chests and pewter. The minstrels' gallery is enclosed, with arched openings for the music to escape.

The drawing room is adorned with paintings by Herring and Opie, including one of the many Opie self-portraits. The Great Chamber above is the glory of Trerice, the ceiling presumably by the same hand as the Great Hall, with a swaggering barrel vault. A wide bow window overlooks the garden. An Aubusson tapestry fills the end wall.

Trerice is not a big house. A gallery passes along the back of the Great Hall to what would have been the kitchen wing. This part of the house, long abandoned, was rebuilt in the 1950s, its 17th-century furniture and landscapes then introduced. This is a charming place. Here I encountered that rare sight, a National Trust guardian snoozing in a side room in the heat of a warm day. I sympathized, and tiptoed out.

Below The Great Hall at Trerice rises through two storeys to a splendid plasterwork ceiling. Ribbing weaves its way across the surface of the ceiling to form geometrical patterns. Oak leaves and scrollwork decorate the design and converging lines of ribbing are finished with dramatic globular pendants. The initials J.A., K.A. and M.A., found among the ornament, are probably those of Sir John Arundell, his wife Katherine and his sister Margaret.

Trewithen

★ ★ An early Georgian house with a Rococo saloon and magnificent garden

6 miles E of Truro; private house and garden, open part year

The lawn at Trewithen glides away from the south front, divided by tapering walls of rhododendrons, magnolias and camellias. In spring it looks like a rend in a coat of many colours. The botanical riches imported by returning British voyagers from the Orient is here on full display.

The house was begun in 1715 by Philip Hawkins. The present structure was largely the work of Philip's executors in 1738–40 for his nephew, Thomas Hawkins, who became the local MP. Thomas married Anne Heywood, daughter of a London merchant, who brought with her dowry the best of metropolitan taste. The house had to respond.

The architect is documented as Thomas Edwards, but Hawkins is believed to have employed Sir Robert Taylor for the main reception rooms along the south front. Thomas was a public-spirited figure who tried to persuade his tenants to use the new smallpox vaccine. He did so by using it on himself, the example losing some force when he died of the illness.

The house has a plain early-Georgian plan, a rectangular building with flanking pavilions. The entrance front is rendered and rather dull. Not so the interior. The house is still occupied by Hawkins descendants, a continuity reflected in the pictures, furniture, books and objects that crowd the rooms shown to visitors. The chief room on the south front is the saloon, presumably the epitome of Anne's sophistication. It is screened at each end by pillars forming a vaulted recess. Soft green walls are offset by fine Rococo plasterwork. The fireplace is a swirling mass of curves. This must have seemed more than refreshing in a land of solid Jacobean panelling and heraldic overmantels.

The drawing room is panelled in varying shades of yellow. Here are portraits by Opie, including his favourite subject, himself. The study panelling is unpainted, with fluted pilasters, and the room has glorious views of the garden. In the rear hall is a modern mural of the Trewithen estate, now owned by the Galsworthy family. The garden was created by the Edwardian owner, George Johnstone.

In the saloon, the stucco decoration around the fireplace rises up the wall above the mantel to create a Rococo wreath picture frame. The portrait – painted by John Vanderbanke, a fashionable London artist of the day – is of Philip Hawkins who began the building of Trewithen in 1715.

Compton Castle

Devon

Devon

A la Ronde

★ ★ ★ A Georgian ladies' 'cabinet of curiosities'

At Exmouth, 6 miles SW of Exeter; National Trust, open part year

Two cousins, Jane and Mary Parminter, returned in 1798 from the Grand Tour in Italy. They were overloaded not with great art – they were not rich – but with what today would be considered up-market souvenirs.

One cousin died in 1811 and the other in 1849. They insisted in their wills that the house be kept intact for ever and inherited only by an 'unmarried kinswoman'. A clergyman descendant broke this trust in the 1890s, enlarging the drawing room and installing a central heating system. On his death, his wife then tried to sell the house (proving the old ladies' point). It was recovered by another female relative and opened to the public in 1935. The National Trust acquired it in 1991.

Partly designed by the Parminter ladies, on a plan inspired by the church of San Vitale in Ravenna, and partly by a cousin from Bath, A la Ronde is one of the most eccentric houses in England. It is sixteen-sided with a conical roof. This was originally thatched and without the present dormer windows. The result, it was said, 'would not be out of place in one of the South Sea Islands'.

A la Ronde today cuts a sad figure in suburban Exmouth. Its charm deserves better surroundings than a sea of bungalows, pubs and used-car dealers. Only from an upstairs window can one look out over the Exe to the Haldon Hills beyond and sense the Devonian grandeur sought by the two ladies as fit setting for their youthful memories.

'A la Ronde is a **tiny jewel** in the National Trust **crown.**'

Above On their Grand Tour of Italy in the late 1790s, the Parminter cousins visited the 6th-century Byzantine church of San Vitale in Ravenna. This octagonal church, by an unknown architect, left its mark and inspired them in the building of A la Ronde. Although the exterior of A la Ronde actually has sixteen sides, at its heart on the inside is this symmetrical, eight-sided hall.

The building's exterior is polygonal, its oddity accentuated by lozenge-shaped windows. Inside, the plan leads to awkward chambers with even more awkward alcoves between them. The rooms radiate from a central octagon, rising to a lantern lined with a collection of shells. This phenomenon is reached up a 'grotto' stair, also lined with shells and too fragile to be accessible. The ladies were shell-mad.

Yet structure at A la Ronde is subordinate to content. The interior is a shrine to the taste of a period and of the Parminter cousins. They collected mostly inconsequential oddments but were skilled craftswomen and mounted and displayed the objects with panache. They were proficient at needlework, drawing, woodturning and collage.

Above The walls of the shell gallery are completely covered with patterns made up of feathers, shells and quillwork. Shell grottos were not uncommon in the 18th and 19th centuries, but since most were built outside few have survived with their decoration as intact as it is at A la Ronde. **Below** Yet more collections of shells fill display cabinets and cupboards; many, like these cowries, were brought back from far-flung shores.

Their dexterity with shells was amazing. The drawing room fireplace is a composition reminiscent of the English surrealist, Tristram Hillier. The shell gallery and its cases are a feast of scallops, conchs, quills, feathers, mica, glass, stones and bones.

The gallery and the staircase to it form the most complete example of the art of feather, shell and quillwork in England, possibly anywhere. Usually such compositions simply disintegrate. Here the pieces were fixed to card before being set in wet plaster on the walls. The shell gallery was conceived as a Gothick fantasy, with pointed arches and vaults encrusted with shells and feather, reflected in small mirrors. In the gallery itself is a clerestory of painted windows within shell-encrusted recesses. This is now so fragile that it can only be seen on a video screen downstairs.

All the rooms are crowded. There are numerous pictures of the ladies and their relatives, including a charming silhouette of them in the drawing room. This room contains a remarkable 'feather frieze', made of the plumage of native game birds and chickens. In the study is a beautifully embroidered coverlet and in the music room a piano which visitors are allowed to play. A la Ronde is a tiny jewel in the National Trust crown.

Arlington court

★★☆ Classical house with a woodland garden and an Edwardian lady's collection

At Arlington, 7 miles NE of Barnstaple; National Trust, house open part year, grounds all year

Never did the outside of a house so belie the inside. The walk from the car park at Arlington Court passes a cold grey façade fronted by a semi-circular Doric portico. Ring to enter, says a rather forbidding notice. I felt inclined to run. Arlington's cellars are known to possess bats with the highest frequency sound pulses in Britain.

In 1820, Colonel John Chichester commissioned a Barnstaple man, Thomas Lee, to build him a villa on a wooded Exmoor hillside over the River Yeo. Lee had worked briefly in John Soane's office, an influence evident inside.

Colonel Chichester's grandson was a high-living grandee who married Rosalie Chamberlayne, daughter of a yachting family. They had one child, a daughter, also Rosalie, much of whose life appears to have been spent on the family yacht, *Erminia*.

Chichester died of Maltese fever in 1881 and his wife remarried and 'went off'. The twenty-year-old Rosalie was left alone with the house, living there and caring for it for almost seventy years, latterly with her companion, Chrissy Peters. She died in 1949, when the house passed to the National Trust.

What one sees today is as it was left by Rosalie. The interior is architecturally simple, as befits a student of Soane, but decorated and furnished in *grande dame* style. At its core is a hall and spacious staircase, off which the principal rooms all lead. The three main reception rooms are divided only by screens of columns, their ceilings delicate and Soanian.

Rosalie Chichester's personality dominates every corner. She was a true lord of the manor. She regularly entertained her tenants and local schoolchildren, founded the local Primrose

League, published the local newspaper, wrote for the *Daily Sketch* and, during the Second World War, ran the local Land Army. She guarded the Yeo valley with her life. It was declared a nature reserve and nobody was allowed to cut down a single tree. Birds were everywhere, including in the house, which became an informal aviary.

Above all, Chichester collected. She collected constantly, globally and indiscriminately, like the earlier Parminters of A la Ronde (see page 60). She particularly liked shells and animal statues. With Chrissy Peters, she travelled the world and returned with trunk-loads of souvenirs. The two of them appear photographed in distant parts in heavy tweed skirts, sensible shoes, hat and stick. They look more than a match for any Levantine guide.

A list of these contents is near pointless. What is remarkable is the flair that Chichester brought to displaying her acquisitions. The objects are arranged in formal patterns, mostly in cases. In the morning room are ships and shells. The ante-room was for canaries, of which

Left The Morning Room, some 70ft (21m) long, has three distinct areas; by placing screens between the pairs of scagliola columns the room could be divided into three smaller rooms. It was originally a dining room but came to be used as a Morning Room to take advantage of the easterly aspect. **Above** In the Boudoir, the mirrored corners are framed by Italianate pilasters that were added in the late 19th century. The rose-and-gold silk wall coverings and the plasterwork ceiling were part of the original design by Thomas Lee.

'Never did the outside

Above Part of the stable block at Arlington is used to display horse-drawn carriages from the National Trust's collection. Around 50 different vehicles have been brought together, some from other Trust properties, others loaned or donated by private individuals or other institutions. Various harnesses and other equipment are also on show. Among the grandest carriages are Lord Craven's State Chariot of 1850, and a State Coach from Knole, in Kent, of 1860.

sadly none survive or has been replaced. The White Drawing Room has an amber elephant and a huge conch shell on which it is tempting to blow.

Beyond the reception rooms are subsidiary collections. The music room contains pots given to Chichester in appreciation of her help in funding the archaeological dig at Ur. A jigsaw puzzle is left on a table for visitors to help complete, a nice touch in an otherwise don't-touch house. The hall is filled with pictures of yachts, parrots and paintings of the house by Peters.

The upstairs bedrooms have been Trustified. Even the clutter seems to have been arranged by a committee. No speck of dust would dare show its face. But the cabinets retain their appeal: a line of elephants in descending order of magnitude, fans and baby costumes, pots and mugs, spoons and ladles, pet mice. The back rooms are even madder. One contains model boats. A cupboard is full of pewter. Shells and coral are everywhere. The visitor may wonder, why? Rosalie Chichester would shrug and say, why not?

Arlington has a spectacular collection of carriages in its stables and a tradition of modern sculpture in its garden.

of a house so belie the inside.'

Berry Pomeroy castle

⋆⋆ The ruin of an Elizabethan house above a ravine

2 miles NE of Totnes; English Heritage, open part year

Berry Pomeroy is reached through dense woodland, its walls braving a ravine above the Gatcombe Brook. The castle of the Norman Pomeroys was one of many properties acquired by Edward Seymour, 1st Duke of Somerset, in 1547, at the height of his power as Protector of England under the infant Edward VI. He converted it as a local residence in Elizabethan style. After his fall, his grandson retreated to Devon and made Berry Pomeroy his home, rebuilding the Great Hall range, *c*1600, and giving it a grand Renaissance façade to the courtyard. The castle was abandoned at the end of the 17th century.

The castle enclosure is reached through a large gatehouse with polygonal turrets. This is still intact. Its upper chamber appears to have been a chapel, with arcade, small aisle and wall-paintings of the Adoration of the Three Kings. Above it are guardrooms. To the right of the gate is the surviving wall walk of the old castle, offering excellent views over the ruins of the interior, beyond which lies the spectacular ravine.

These ruins face into the courtyard. To the right is the earlier range built by Seymour senior, a sumptuous mid-16th-century house in the manner of Hardwick Old Hall (Derbyshire). Its walls stand three storeys high and the façade is roughly symmetrical, with a small courtyard hidden behind. The house has mullioned windows open to the sky, with fireplaces and stairs gazing out into space. It forms a ghostly tableau, as though a backdrop to an Elizabethan drama.

At right angles to this façade and backing directly onto the ravine are the footings of the younger Seymour's house. It had a loggia below and two storeys of glazed windows above. Behind would have been the Great Hall, with the kitchens and services to the left.

If Pomeroy were mine, I would be tempted to rebuild it. The property belongs to the Duke of Somerset and is displayed by English Heritage. It would make a spectacular house and a sensational hotel, with nothing to lose but a few ghosts. The Victorians missed a trick.

Bickleigh castle

 A medieval gatehouse with 17th-century wing

At Bickleigh, 3 miles S of Tiverton; private house, open by arrangement

The old tower sits on the banks of the River Exe below Tiverton. The rest of the medieval Bickleigh was destroyed by Cromwell's troops on their rampage through the West Country in the 1640s, but a new wing was built, or rebuilt, shortly afterwards, yielding today's L-shaped house. Created by the Courtenays and held until 1926 by the Carews, it is now privately owned.

The gatehouse façade to the river is unusually wide, indicating what must have been a large Elizabethan house behind. The windows are mostly Tudor, earlier on the ground floor. The central arch has a fine ribbed vault. To its left is the old armoury, filled with Cromwellian weaponry. A set of stone relief carvings form an overmantel in the drawing room. They appear to show scenes from the suppression of the anti-Reformation Prayer Book Rebellion of 1549 outside Exeter; it is a work of great historical importance.

To the right of the arch are conventional Carew portraits and an extraordinary picture of Napoleon staring into a fire in the aftermath of Waterloo. An original 14th-century staircase leads to a Great Chamber over the gateway. This has large windows, roaring fires and two full-length Georgian portraits of John and Elizabeth Carew. In the Jacobean wing is a dining room, heavy with beams and pewter. Above is a bedroom with a chunky, probably 16th-century, four-poster.

Right This carved stone panel at Bickleigh is believed to show events from the Prayer Book Rebellion which swept the West Country in 1549, during the reign of Edward VI. The uprising was sparked off by the enforced use of a new prayer book and the abandonment of the old Latin mass. Rebels laid siege to Exeter in Devon for five weeks.

Broadclyst: Marker's cottage

 Medieval thatched cob cottage with painted hall partition

At Broadclyst, 4 miles NE of Exeter; National Trust, open part year

This pretty cottage tucked away in a back street of Broadclyst dates from the 15th century. It is outwardly a simple thatched structure, named after a Georgian owner, Sally Marker. The building has three rooms with a cross passage.

A parlour is formed by a wooden partition dividing the hall in half, apparently to exclude the smoke from a central hearth. This hearth was replaced by a fireplace in the Tudor period. A later rear stair turret led to a new upper room created in the roof, with dormer windows. All this reflects the customary modernization of medieval houses in the 16th century. The cottage belongs to the National Trust.

The delight of Marker's is the hall partition, covered on both sides by thick layers of paint. On the hall side, where the fire was located, the paintings are barely discernible but they combine abstract patterns with figures. On the parlour side is a representation of cherubs and of St Andrew with his cross and ship. It displays the sophistication achieved by artisan craftsmen in these out-of-the-way places.

Above The painted hall partition at Marker's cottage is a fine example of a plank-and-muntin wall. Such walls were constructed of a frame of beams, the 'muntins', infilled with panels, the 'planks'. The sturdy wooden beams were usually 8-by-8 inches (20cm) thick.

There is a small chamber above the hall and an original unglazed mullioned window in the lower room, used for storage. These windows were often known as Armada windows, installed as house improvements to celebrate the end of economic uncertainty with the defeat of the Spanish fleet. The Trust has left an old 1950s fireplace, demonstrating the passage of time.

Broomham farm

⭐ A semi-derelict medieval farmhouse, including a stone-and-cob cruck hall

Near King's Nympton, 5 miles S of South Molton; private house, viewed by arrangement

When I approached Broomham Farm its owner, Mr Clements, calmed his ferocious dogs and demanded of me, 'You from Devon?' When I said no, he muttered, 'A furriner!' I told him I was on my way to Cornwall, which he warned me was 'bows and arrows country'. A fine sense of territory is still alive in England.

Few readers will find this place and Mr Clements will not mind. Broomham is in a lost valley between South Molton and King's Nympton. The old buildings are part of a complete medieval group round a Devonian cruck hall, a stone and cob construction with a thatched roof, dating from the 14th century. Its discovery greatly excited English Heritage and a grant has restored the thatch but no more. The house is (or was on my visit) still semi-derelict. The upstairs rooms, last occupied half a century ago, are still filled with old bedsteads, steamer trunks, gas masks and back numbers of *Picture Post*.

The core of the farm is a hall with a later upper storey inserted. To one side is a massive fireplace. Upstairs, the crucks are evident, with plaster still clinging to them in places. The bedrooms are at the family end of the hall, the service range at the other. The latter is a tumbledown storeroom with, behind it, the old kitchen, dairy, pantry and spiral staircase to the attic, where the farmworkers would have slept. The smoking room for curing meat is intact, a great rarity.

A date of 1638 can be discerned on the front of the house, presumably the date of its last 'modernization'. Outside the wall, an old watercourse runs past what would have been the scullery and garderobe. These are all the more remarkable for being covered in dirt and dust, frozen in time, utterly neglected. What is precious about Broomham is not its past but its present, and that cannot last.

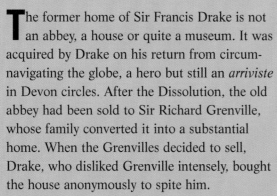

Buckland abbey

★★★ Cistercian abbey converted into Tudor house; home of Francis Drake

★★★ Cistercian abbey converted into Tudor house; home of Francis Drake

5 miles S of Tavistock; National Trust, open part year

The former home of Sir Francis Drake is not an abbey, a house or quite a museum. It was acquired by Drake on his return from circumnavigating the globe, a hero but still an *arriviste* in Devon circles. After the Dissolution, the old abbey had been sold to Sir Richard Grenville, whose family converted it into a substantial home. When the Grenvilles decided to sell, Drake, who disliked Grenville intensely, bought the house anonymously to spite him.

Grenvilles reacquired it after the Civil War a century later, but Drakes repossessed it and held it by descent until 1937. After a severe fire the following year, it was sold to a neighbour who gave it to the National Trust.

The Abbey was a Cistercian foundation, sited with customary seclusion in a curve of the Tavy valley. The Grenvilles did not do what most post-Dissolution occupiers did and demolish the monastery church and use the abbot's quarters

as a residence. They converted the church itself. As a result, ghosts of arcade arches can be seen buried in later walls. Gothic windows are interspersed with Tudor and Georgian ones. Corbels start out of drawing room ceilings.

Tracing the original abbey plan is thus confusing. To make it even harder, parts of the abbey have been converted into private apartments. After descending the valley through charming gardens, visitors enter directly onto a Georgian staircase which rises spectacularly through four floors of the old church. It leads to exhibition galleries inserted horizontally in the volume of the old nave. The upper ones were rebuilt after the 1938 fire. Drake's coat of arms can be seen over the granite fireplace, placed within what was the old crossing arch.

Off the 'nave' galleries are the old family living rooms. The Drake Chamber and the dining room are finely furnished and hung with

Above centre The Great Barn is a surviving relic of the original Cistercian abbey. Probably built around 1300, its size is a clear indication of the wealth of the monastic community; the produce of the Buckland Abbey estates would have been stored within its walls. **Above right** An 18th-century Sir Francis Drake, the 5th Baronet, had this grand staircase installed at Buckland some time during the late 1700s. It rises up through four storeys.

Sir Francis Drake
*c*1540–1596

Francis Drake was born around 1540 in Crowndale, just a few miles from Buckland. In 1549, the uprising known as the Prayer Book Rebellion (see page 67) forced his staunchly Protestant family to flee Devon for Kent. It was from here that Francis first went to sea, aged about 13. In less than 10 years he was master of his own vessel. He sold the ship and returned to Plymouth, from where he sailed on the many voyages that were to bring him fame and fortune. He amassed so much booty during his circumnavigation of the world, in 1577–80, that he was able to buy Buckland Abbey on his return for the then princely sum of £3,400.

Below The trusses supporting the ceiling of Buckland's Great Hall are concealed beneath plasterwork decoration; satyrs bearing shields stand against each truss. The date MCCCCCLXXVI (1576) is incorporated into the frieze above the fireplace. Most of the oak furniture in the room is 16th or 17th century, although there is a 19th-century armchair reputed to have been made of wood taken from Drake's most famous ship *The Golden Hind*.

contemporary paintings, but they are somehow lost in the museum displays. Only the Great Hall truly holds its own, built in the 16th century into the church crossing. This was one of the earlier Grenville family's rooms, dated 1576, and has been restored as such. The plasterwork is original, a didactic display of Elizabethan imagery. Over the fireplace are the four Virtues beneath a bracket of a devilish satyr. The ceiling has geometrical tracery, but at one end a tableau depicts an old soldier retiring to cloistered Buckland and resting under a vine, a charming Virgilian vignette. The wood panelling is equally decorative, with inlaid animal masks and fertility symbols.

Beyond the Great Hall is a chapel created on the site of the Abbey high altar by a Drake descendant, Lady Seaton, in 1917. Outside the house is a knot garden, herb garden and maze of paths. Buckland's most remarkable survival is the Great Barn through which visitors must pass to reach the house. This gigantic structure dates back to the Cistercian period and was reputedly bigger than the Abbey church itself.

Burgh island

 Art Deco pleasure palace on an offshore island

Near Bigbury-on-Sea, 5 miles E of Kingsbridge; now a hotel

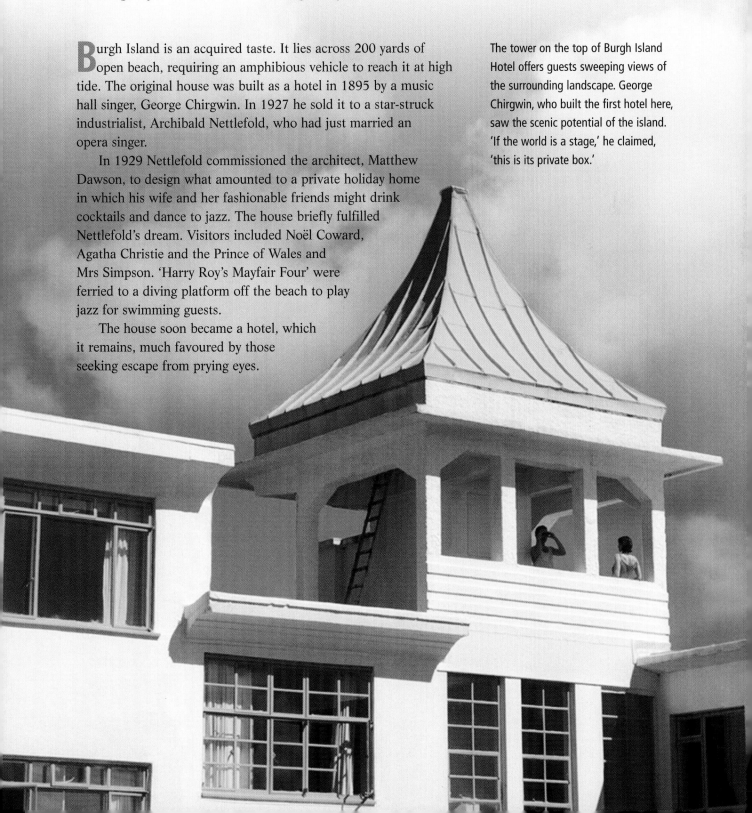

Burgh Island is an acquired taste. It lies across 200 yards of open beach, requiring an amphibious vehicle to reach it at high tide. The original house was built as a hotel in 1895 by a music hall singer, George Chirgwin. In 1927 he sold it to a star-struck industrialist, Archibald Nettlefold, who had just married an opera singer.

In 1929 Nettlefold commissioned the architect, Matthew Dawson, to design what amounted to a private holiday home in which his wife and her fashionable friends might drink cocktails and dance to jazz. The house briefly fulfilled Nettlefold's dream. Visitors included Noël Coward, Agatha Christie and the Prince of Wales and Mrs Simpson. 'Harry Roy's Mayfair Four' were ferried to a diving platform off the beach to play jazz for swimming guests.

The house soon became a hotel, which it remains, much favoured by those seeking escape from prying eyes.

The tower on the top of Burgh Island Hotel offers guests sweeping views of the surrounding landscape. George Chirgwin, who built the first hotel here, saw the scenic potential of the island. 'If the world is a stage,' he claimed, 'this is its private box.'

'Its sleek **white outline** ... stands **bold** against the **green** of the island.'

Agatha Christie
1890–1976

Agatha Christie was born Agatha Miller on 15th September 1890 at Barton Road, Torquay. Her father died while she was still a child and so her mother brought Agatha up on her own in Torquay. Devon was to remain important to the crime writer throughout her life and local landmarks often featured in her novels.

Her first book was *The Mysterious Affair at Styles* (1920); it was also the first to feature her famous creation, the Belgian detective Hercule Poirot. It was Poirot that Agatha Christie sent on holiday to Burgh Island in *Evil Under the Sun* (1941), although in the novel the resort is renamed Smuggler's Island.

Agatha Christie used it as the setting for a number of novels, with television's Poirot following close behind. The building remains a rare example of an Art Deco residence. Its sleek white outline with small tower stands bold against the green of the island. Everything about the place, the doorways, lift, lavatories, even the menus and lettering, is Art Deco, a miniature Savoy.

Of the original rooms, the entrance to the ballroom is the most evocative. It might be the saloon of a Transatlantic liner. The bar has a skylight of stained glass fanning out into a peacock's tail. The hotel walls are decorated with Fritz Lang movie posters, photographs of inter-war movie stars and framed bathing costumes of the period. The dining room has one lapse in taste, a naval bar bought from the last sailing vessel commissioned by the Royal Navy, HMS *Ganges*, broken for scrap in 1929.

Below the hotel, a cluster of fishing cottages survive, together with the admirable Pilchards Inn. 'Imagine a silver shining sea of pilchards frothing to the windward,' enthuses the hotel.

Right Above the Palm Court bar is a stained-glass skylight, patterned in the form of a peacock's tail. The Art Deco styling of this room, and others throughout the hotel, is reminiscent of a 1930s ocean liner, all sleek lines, geometric patterns and lots of polished chrome and glass. It is not hard to imagine famous former guests, such as Noël Coward, Gertrude Lawrence, Jesse Matthews or Amy Johnson, seated in the Lloyd Loom chairs, enjoying a cocktail.

Cadhay

★★★ Tudor house with an inner courtyard featuring Jacobean statues

1 mile NW of Ottery St Mary; private house, open part year

Cadhay is a Tudor house with a simple E-plan façade and inner courtyard, still in private family ownership. The house was mostly built in the 1540s in the traditional form of a hall with screens passage and service and domestic wings behind. The owner was John Haydon, a lawyer who grew rich dissolving monasteries in the West Country. His great-nephew, Robert, enclosed the three ranges with a Long Gallery, forming an inner courtyard.

This courtyard is the pride of the house. It is symmetrical, with statues of Henry VIII and his three monarch offspring, Edward, Mary and Elizabeth, adorning each façade. The stonework is laid chequerboard, of limestone interspersed with local 'chert' flint. Called the Court of Sovereigns, it is one of the treasures of Devon. The statues, erected in 1617, are wonderfully accomplished works of

Right and far left The statues that give the inner courtyard its name, the Court of Sovereigns, were probably put up in 1617. Each wall of the courtyard bears an elaborately decorated niche housing a statue. The four statues are representations of Henry VIII (far left) and his three children, Edward VI, Mary I and Elizabeth I (right), who ruled England in succession after Henry's death. The date 1617 can be seen just below the niche that holds the figure of Elizabeth.

Jacobean Mannerism. The figures seem to burst from their niches between complex classical columns on ornamental brackets. The carver is unknown.

Cadhay was converted internally by a new owner, William Peere Williams, in 1736. Its charm now lies in the marriage of these two periods. Williams altered many of the rooms and put an upper floor in the Great Hall. The house was later rescued from agricultural use by a Cambridge academic, Dampier Whetham, who bought Cadhay in 1910 and reinstated its Tudor character in line with the Edwardian revival of interest in English vernacular. Beyond the Great Hall, where the solar range would have been, are family living rooms. The Williams-Powlett family have owned the house since 1935.

Upstairs and at the rear of the inner courtyard is the Long Gallery. The old barrel vault is plastered and the room filled not with pictures but with odds and ends of family history. A collection of pewter finds space among bits of furniture, pistols and books about Devonian fly-fishing. The chamber above the Great Hall shows its original roof: great curved beams, braces and rafters much abused by time but the nobler for it. Cadhay has an enjoyably faded domesticity. It is warmed by oil heaters only. Cobwebs guard the rafters.

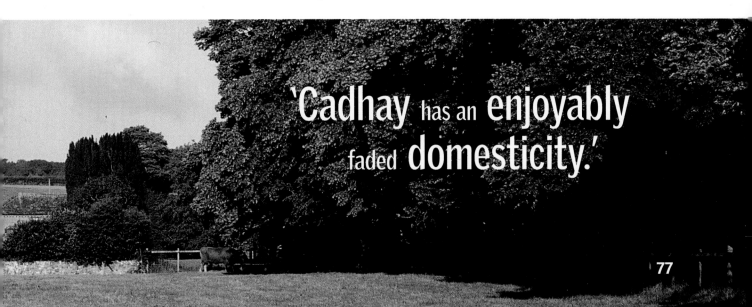

'Cadhay has an enjoyably faded domesticity.'

Castle **Drogo**

Castle Drogo is a monument to one man's pride. Julius Drew ranked with Thomas Lipton and John Sainsbury as one of the kings of Victorian retailing. In 1883, at the age of just thirty-three, he was so rich he retired from his Home and Colonial Stores empire and set up as a country gentleman. Born of a line of merchants, he married well and bought Wadhurst Hall in Sussex. By 1900 he was a JP and appeared in *Burke's Landed Gentry* as 'Drew of Wadhurst Hall'. Neither Lipton nor Sainsbury was listed, much to his satisfaction.

Drew set about acquiring a pedigree to match his wealth, with a determination normally confined to the immigrant rich. He traced the Drew family to Devon and possibly to a Norman knight called Drogo, and added an -e to his name in the process. Land was acquired in the vicinity of the conveniently named Drewsteignton. Finally in 1910 Edwin Lutyens was commissioned to build a castle appropriate to so ancient a line. But even Drewe's reach proved more than his architect's grasp.

The moorland site was and is magnificent. It overlooks the gorge of the River Teign towards the uplands of Dartmoor. The castle was intended to be vast, with barbican, gatehouse, Great Hall and courtyards. Only a third of this was built, and that required twenty years of effort and agony. By the time Castle Drogo was partly finished in 1925, the cost had risen threefold. Drewe had had a stroke and lost his eldest son in the Great War. He died in 1931. Over the door, with its working portcullis, he could see the heraldic 'Drewe lion', but there was not so much as a knighthood to his name. His family passed the house to the National Trust in 1974.

Castle Drogo is a 20th-century palace piled on a rock. It is built of local granite, which is highly porous and prone to leakage. Drewe refused normal drainage pipes, sloping roofs or

Right The library and billiard room at Castle Drogo are part of one large L-shaped room, an arrangement which was popular with the Drewe family who often took afternoon tea here. There was also a wireless and table football game in the room – something to keep everyone amused. Although the large fireplace adds a cosy touch, it isn't all that practical when it comes to warming the room as the door needs to be kept open to prevent the fire from smoking.

Right Lutyens paid just as much attention to the domestic areas of Castle Drogo as to the grand reception rooms, creating this light and imposing kitchen. Scullery maids would have stood at the three large sinks set beneath the plate racks to wash the dishes. Lutyens also included the enormous hexagonal chopping board, seen in the foreground, and a massive pestle and mortar set against the two granite columns.

central heating. This was to be a medieval castle. But Castle Drogo is not a Victorian pastiche. It is unmistakably a 20th-century variation on a medieval theme, and unmistakably Lutyens.

The castle is not a lovable building. Even today, its stone oxidized and bleached with mortar, it seems spartan. Lutyens struggled to give it eccentricity and a sense of humour. The portcullis grins, the south-east tower has medieval 'beaks' or batwings to resist sappers. But the jokes are forced. It is hard to imagine a young family bouncing about the place, relaxing and cracking jokes. Dressing for dinner at Castle Drogo would imply a suit of armour.

Severity is at least relieved by furniture and fittings. Many were acquired by Drewe from a bankrupt Spanish banker, from whom he had bought Wadhurst. They are anything but 'ancestral' and give the entrance an Iberian feel.

The library and billiard room contain tapestries from Wadhurst and are warmed by large Axminster carpets, something of a relief. The shelves were not fitted until 1931, the year of Drewe's death. In the library is a German table football machine of 1900. The drawing room, with its deal panelled walls and chintz chair covers, has large windows filling it with light and views.

The rest of the castle is a warren of stone corridors and barrel vaults. A staircase of spacious proportions, lit by a huge window, leads down to a modest dining room. This was Lutyens' eventual substitute for the original Great Hall and Great Chamber, intended for this range. The room is 17th century in style, panelled and with a rich plaster ceiling. The Lutyens signature is a bare granite frieze through which water would regularly leak. Once when

Above In comfortable contrast to the grand reception rooms, this family bedroom has a more intimate feel, due in part to the lower ceiling and softer furnishings. Below The pantry remains very much as it would have been in Julius Drewe's day. On one wall is the bell board that indicated which room required the attendance of a servant. On the adjacent wall is the telephone exchange which linked the castle's 18 telephones to the outside world.

dining at Castle Drogo, Lutyens drew pictures on his menu card, mixing mustard and wine for ink.

Despite its structural medievalism, Castle Drogo was and is full of modern appliances. A built-in vacuum cleaning system sucked dirt from the floors into wall vents. There were 332 electric sockets and a superb and complex switchroom. The domestic wing is modest, almost comfortable. A room is kept as memorial to the young Adrian Drewe, killed at Ypres. A charming chapel was constructed in the undercroft of the south wing.

When asked about a garden, Julius Drewe told Lutyens that he wanted 'heather, bracken, broom, holly, brambles, foxgloves'. He got them. This is a Dartmoor landscape of pines and tors, rocky outcrops and sweeps of moorland. Yet a formal garden was designed out of sight of the moorland vista, to the north-west, advised by Gertrude Jekyll. It is a pleasant enclave, quite inappropriate to a castle.

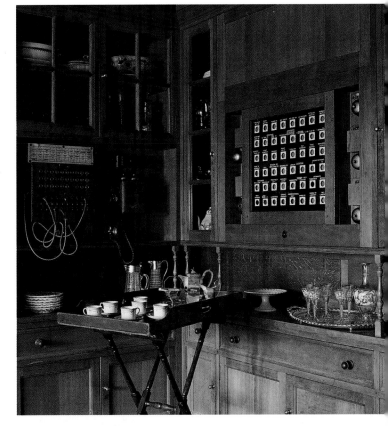

Above Great care has been taken to furnish the kitchen of this fisherman's cottage with appropriate items. A tin bath sits in front of the range and socks are hung out to dry above it. The cooking utensils on the table give the impression of a meal in preparation.

Clovelly:
Fisherman's
cottage

⭐ Simple cottage in a picturesque village

At Clovelly, 10 miles W of Bideford; museum, open all year

The former fishing village of Clovelly clinging to its cliff in North Devon is still worth a detour. I say this despite the locating of a large supermarket and visitor 'experience' on the hillside above it. This is to enable the Rous estate, owners of the village, to charge visitors for access. Most such owners might make do with a car park kiosk. As it is, the centre has stolen the village tourist trade.

The main street down to the harbour remains charming, rejoicing in the name, 'Up along down along'. The initials CH on many cottages indicate the year of their renovation under a previous benefactress, Christina Hamlyn. Behind the former house of the writer, Charles Kingsley, is a small cottage restored as that of a Victorian fisherman, although its last occupant was Mrs Webber, the village seamstress.

The conversion has been well done. Downstairs is a sitting room and kitchen-cum-bathroom. Upstairs is a single and a double bedroom, with space in the loft for drying sails, nets and other fishing paraphernalia. On the walls hang simple Biblical texts. Oilskins and old sweaters droop from pegs. Photographs convey some sense of the tight-knit community which inhabited the place from the late 1500s into the 20th century.

Coleton Fishacre

★★ 'Jazz-age' holiday house with Art Deco interiors

3½ miles E of Dartmouth; National Trust, open part year

The new rich of the 20th century may have had style, but they rarely had longevity. They built their country houses as retreats, used them for a while and lost interest. Their children felt no bond with county England.

Coleton was built by Rupert D'Oyly Carte, son of the impresario of the Gilbert and Sullivan operas and proprietor of the Savoy Theatre and Hotel. A fashionable young man (his elder brother, Lucas, was said to be the model for Wodehouse's Psmith), he married the daughter of the Earl of Cranbrook. He and his wife selected the site for their new country house from a yacht offshore, hardly a sign of commitment to the land.

The house was built in 1923–6 and claims to be a 'house of the jazz age'. Yet the exterior is firmly in the manorial vernacular style of the Arts and Crafts movement. It has sweeping gabled roofs, stone walls and small chimneys.

Coleton Fishacre's architect was Oswald Milne, who had worked in Lutyens' office and was shortly to be displaced at neighbouring Dartington for designing in an 'Early Georgian and vernacular' style that was considered 'out of keeping with [Dartington's] modern needs', as the guidebook puts it.

The site is gloriously isolated, at the end of a long lane that seems never to reach the sea. The polygonal entrance porch fills the angle of what is a 'butterfly' house, a plan favoured by early 20th-century architects. The interior is essentially a stage-set for entertaining. The entrance hall leads directly into the saloon, reached down a semi-circular flight of steps beneath an Art Deco arch. We can imagine new arrivals alighting from their Bentleys and finding themselves suddenly 'on parade' at the top of the steps. This spectacular room has a plastered ceiling, its emptiness relieved by Art Deco wall lights. The rugs are by the American designer, Marion Dorn.

The saloon is complemented by a sitting room, library and dining room, some with original fittings. Upstairs are Edward Bawden tiles in the bathrooms, honeycomb ceiling lights but as yet little furniture. Many views to the sea, such as from the dining loggia, have become obscured by trees. Such landscaping is baffling. Surely vistas intended by architects should be respected as such.

Rupert's son was killed in a car accident and his daughter Bridget sold the house in 1949. It passed to the National Trust in 1982, along with a spectacular stretch of coastline desperately in need of protection, and admirable gardens open to the public.

Combe house

Left The Great Hall is now one of the hotel's reception rooms at Combe House. Despite the dark wood panelling around the walls, the room remains light and bright, enlivened by the simple decoration on the plasterwork ceiling. Corinthian pilasters above the fireplace are ornamented with fine carving.

⭐ A neo-Jacobean house set in parkland

At Gittisham, 2 miles SW of Honiton; now a hotel

The winding drive through the woods from Gittisham gives way to parkland across which is seen a fine Jacobean façade against a backdrop of deepest green. The old house was bought in 1615 by a lawyer, Nicholas Putt, whose descendant, Thomas Putt, restored it after 1815. It is now carefully neo-Jacobean, with a picturesque flurry of gables and chimneys. The house is a discreet hotel.

The old Great Hall is still that, a high, bold chamber of the late 17th century with surprisingly grand bolection moulded panelling. Doorcases have big broken pediments and the fireplace is flanked by pilasters and carved fruit. Walls are deep crimson, adorned with stags' heads and old portraits. This room is almost ducal in scale.

Two other reception rooms merit attention. The dining room is decorated with recently painted rustic murals. Its neighbour, another dining room, is an amazing survival. Decorated in the 18th century, it is alive with English Rococo plasterwork. The overmantel carries fronds and Ho-Ho birds, themes repeated in high relief in the ceiling. The doorcases are likewise decorated with birds. The room is gay and lighthearted.

Combe House shows how a hotel, sensitively handled, can bring life to an old house. There is a log fire in the grate, a burst of flowers on every plinth, a fine staircase and little sign of commercialism.

Compton castle

✦ ✦ ✦ A complete medieval fortified manor

At Compton, 4 miles W of Torquay; National Trust, open part year

This might be a set design for a Disney epic. Yet Compton is the real thing, a medieval fortified manor with its defences intact. The north front lies in a Devon combe beyond a long, thatched barn. Although the house belongs to the National Trust, it is still occupied and maintained by its ancestral owners, the Gilberts.

The old manor was begun in the 14th century, when a Compton married a Gilbert. A later Gilbert added the surrounding curtain wall in the 1520s, whether from genuine fear of attack or antiquarian ostentation, we do not know. The answer by that date was almost certainly the latter.

The Gilberts abandoned Compton in the 1800s and it fell into ruin. Pictures of the house in the late 19th century show a mirage of a castle enveloped in creeper, like something from Angkor Wat. This ruin was reacquired in 1930 by the splendidly named Commander Walter Raleigh Gilbert, who restored it as a family home. This it remains.

'... Compton is the real thing, a medieval, fortified manor ...'

The restored house is complete in all essentials. A high wall encloses a tight inner courtyard. The house itself is H-plan round the Great Hall, reconstructed in 1955 on archaeological evidence, with decorated tracery in the windows. A small garden lies within the walls to the rear.

Compton is more modest than it seems from outside. On one side of the Great Hall is a solar above an old cellar, refashioned as a parlour. In front of it is a small chapel, still in use. On the other side is the steward's room, buttery, pantry, larder and kitchen. The last is a magnificent survival, with plaster crumbling over rough stone and one of the biggest fireplaces anywhere. Bedrooms were and still are confined to the five enclosing towers, a residence compact and defensible. There are even crossbow slits in the tower rooms.

The present Gilberts have refurnished the house in the Tudor style and with mementos of the family through history. Sir Walter Raleigh's mother was a Gilbert by a previous marriage, and Gilberts have long been prominent seamen. They furnished ships to fight the Armada and colonists to populate the American colonies, founding the Canadian province of Newfoundland. A Gilbert son continues the tradition by being called Walter Raleigh.

Above A squirrel features on the Gilbert family crest and there are images of squirrels all over Compton, such as this one on a pew end in the chapel. The *Squirrel* was Sir Humphrey Gilbert's ship on which he returned from Newfoundland. Sadly, the ship sunk off the Azores and he was drowned.
Right The kitchen has changed little since it was added to the castle in the 1520s. The enormous fireplace, some 15ft (4.5m) across, has three flues and bread ovens on either side.

Dartington hall

⋆⋆ A medieval house round a courtyard with restored Great Hall

At Dartington, 2 miles NW of Totnes; private house and gardens, open for external viewing all year, interior viewing by arrangement

Dartington is now the centre of a thriving arts foundation, embracing a summer school, a musical education project, and farming, forestry and conservation enterprises. At the heart of the estate is the old medieval house, arranged round a traditional courtyard, a rare survival from the pre-Tudor era and dating from the end of the 14th century. It was one of the largest such establishments in the West Country and reflects its medieval ownership by the Earl of Huntingdon and by Margaret Beaufort, mother of Henry VII.

In 1559, Dartington was bought by the Champernownes and remained in that family until 1925, when it was sold to Leonard and Dorothy Elmhirst. Leonard was a Yorkshire squire's son and follower of the Indian poet and progressive reformer, Rabindranath Tagore. Dorothy was daughter of the American tycoon, William Whitney. With this mix of idealism and money, Dartington could not fail.

The semi-derelict medieval buildings were taken in hand by the Elmhirsts and restored with more than usual rigour. The Great Hall had no roof or windows and the porch tower was about to collapse. Pevsner pondered whether the result is not 'more ideal to the American rather than the sloppier British' taste in renovation.

The courtyard is reached through a gate next to the old tithe barn. The original builder, Huntingdon, was executed in 1400, before he could build the customary ostentatious gatehouse. The main ranges are mostly of the late 14th century.

Of the heavily restored interiors only the Great Hall is accessible or of particular interest. It compares with Penshurst (Kent) among the great private halls of its time, but has none of Penshurst's atmosphere. It was restored in the 1920s by William Weir with new roof timbers from the estate. The form is hammerbeam with wind-braces. The giant window openings are worthy of a cathedral although the Gothic tracery is 18th century. The fireplace against the far wall is original. The screen is of the 1920s.

The west range of the courtyard is a rare survival of medieval guests' lodgings, in five groups with four rooms to each group. Such buildings would have housed visitors and the lord's retinue when he was in residence. The barn was converted into a theatre in 1933 by Walter Gropius.

Dartington High Cross house

A leading monument to Modernist architecture

At Dartington, 2 miles NW of Totnes; museum, open part year

High Cross is one of England's few Modern Movement houses accessible to the public. The house was built in 1932 by the Dartington Hall Trust for the headmaster of its school, an American named William Curry. It expressed the latest in Modernist design. To the apostle of that age, Nikolaus Pevsner, High Cross could not have been more exciting, 'one of the first essays in the International Modern Style' in England.

The house was designed by William Lescaze, a Swiss-American whom Curry had used for a house at his previous school in Philadelphia. It showed no respect for Devon, for its materials or climate. 'Smooth-pressed steel doorcases' were imported from America. Nor did it defer to the vernacular tradition of which Dartington was an ideological offshoot, the Arts and Crafts movement. Oswald Milne, architect of traditionalist Coleton Fishacre (see page 83), was sacked to make way for Lescaze.

The house is composed of two linked flat-topped boxes. To the road, a blank wall is relieved only by two decks of horizontal slit windows and a projecting porch. The garden front is more developed, a curved study and three-storey domestic wing. There is a roof terrace outside the master bedroom, for healthy outdoor sleeping. The windows are all metal and, where appropriate, curve round corners in the Bauhaus manner. The render is white, except the garage and guest wing where it is blue.

Curry eulogized the interiors as having 'serenity, clarity and a kind of openness', which he contrasted with houses 'crowded with furniture and knick-knacks'. All lighting is concealed. Fireplaces have dark tiled surrounds. Nothing is superfluous or cosy.

The house was greeted with enthusiasm by the Trust's co-founder, Dorothy Elmhirst, who found it 'stark and beautiful ... I wonder whether in a few years we shall regard every other type of architecture stuffy, suffocating and artificial.'

Although much used for public housing projects, the style was little imitated in domestic architecture, at least when residents were allowed to choose for themselves. Cement and metal do not age or wear well. High Cross seems unable to carry its years, despite efforts to maintain the house's exterior and garden.

Contemplating High Cross today, we can see it only as a blind alley. Yet the house has been well restored for the Dartington archive and marks a chapter in English architectural history.

Below High Cross House was the height of modernity when it was completed in 1932. Its architect, William Lescaze, took as much care designing the interiors as he did the exterior of the building. He picked out the furnishings and decorative finishes to be used, often choosing bold paint colours for certain walls. William Curry, the house's first resident, appreciated its startling modernity: 'I always come back to it with a real sense of relief after having visited a more old fashioned house.'

Endsleigh house

⭐ Regency hunting lodge overlooking a ravine

6 miles NW of Tavistock; now a hotel

In a county of landscape drama, Endsleigh is supreme. On a bright April day the banks of rhododendron escort the visitor to a terraced garden and look-out over the ravine of the River Tamar far below. On every side is thick evergreen. This could be the Hudson River at the time of the early explorers. The estate was crafted by Humphry Repton in 1814 for the 6th Duke of Bedford, of whose Devonian properties Endsleigh forms part (recalled by name in his Bloomsbury streets). When Repton gave the Duke the relevant Red Book he added, 'I confess I never so well pleased myself.'

Above this setting is a Regency hunting lodge. Its site had originally appealed to the Duchess of Bedford, Georgiana, whose four sons laid the foundation stone of the house in 1810.

While Repton planned the landscape, Sir Jeffry Wyatville designed a house and garden buildings. The front courtyard embraced stables and outbuildings and the main house was called Endsleigh Cottage, now House.

The house has been a private fishing club and public restaurant. It is as Wyatville left it, with an entrance hall and suite of reception rooms enjoying superb views over the ravine. The house is furnished as an Edwardian sporting retreat. Old pictures are yellow with age, as is the wallpaper. Trophies peer down from dark ceilings. Battered books in sombre bookcases record sporting achievements on river and moor. The place is of a piece and should not be changed. It is being converted as a hotel at the time of writing.

Fursdon house

⯪ ⯪ An old family house with Georgian façade

6 miles S of Tiverton; private house and garden, open part year

The old walls of Fursdon House have sheltered twenty-three generations of Fursdons in unbroken male succession since the 13th century. Given the present family's fecundity, there seems no danger of the habit being broken. The house is beautifully positioned looking over the Exe Valley towards Dartmoor.

Fursdon was rebuilt in 1732 with a severe, rendered Georgian façade. This was amended in 1818 when George Fursdon returned a hero from the Battle of Waterloo and rewarded himself with a new ballroom and library in one, thus satisfying his twin enthusiasms for dancing and reading. He also constructed a pleasant colonnade across the front. Virginia creeper has since added a further softening touch.

Inside, the former Great Hall has had its old screen restored at one end. The parlour to the left of the entrance has Jacobean panelling,

imported from elsewhere, complete with a scrollwork frieze and caryatids above the fireplace. The staircase hall is hung with pictures of Fursdons throughout history.

The family have assembled the produce of their attics into a small museum to the rear of the ground floor. This includes costumes, weapons and other family paraphernalia. It must have been as enjoyable for the family to assemble as for visitors to enjoy. It is something many houses might copy.

Below This ornamented frieze, supported by four carved caryatids, stands above the fireplace in the parlour at Fursdon. Above each caryatid figure is a shield, each one decorated with a different heraldic device. The coats of arms belong to previous generations of the Fursdon family, further evidence of their long lineage.

Haldon belvedere

The Haldon Hills above the Exe Valley formed a geographical barrier beyond Exeter. They forced even Brunel into a detour, taking his Great Western Railway along the coast at Teignmouth. From the top is a view to Dartmoor, Exmoor, and east to Portland Bill. Small wonder Georgian enthusiasts for the Picturesque could not resist erecting a look-out point on this spot.

Haldon Belvedere is a three-sided Gothick tower, castellated and rendered white. The tower was created in honour of the friendship of two employees of the East India Company, Stringer Lawrence and Sir Robert Palk. Lawrence was an old general who went out to India in 1747 to found the company's militia and form what became the Indian Army. Palk was the company chaplain who renounced holy orders and rose to become Governor of Madras and hugely rich. He returned to England in 1767, married and bought Haldon House (demolished in 1920) with 11,000 acres.

In 1788 Palk built the Belvedere tower as a memorial to his friendship with the general, by then deceased. He called it Lawrence Castle and set a statue of Lawrence in Roman attire in the downstairs hall. It is a Coade stone copy of one by Scheemakers in the Foreign Office in London. The tower above is remarkably handsome. Triangular in plan it has a turret at each angle. One contains a spiral staircase, reputedly the longest continuous cantilever in existence (a frequent claim). There are three floors and a roof terrace. Windows and glazing bars are Gothick. The tower has been well restored by a local trust.

The first floor is a miniature ballroom with parquet floor and Gothick plaster vault. Tripartite windows light each side. Above is a holiday flat with kitchen and bathroom in the turrets. The views on a fine day are spectacular.

Hartland abbey

★★★ Gothick mansion with Victorian interiors by Sir Gilbert Scott

12 miles W of Bideford; private house and gardens, open part year

Hartland Abbey seems at the end of the world. The adjacent coast was a sailor's hell, a place of wrecks, smugglers and hidden coves. The old abbey survived until the Dissolution after which it was given to Henry VIII's wine cellarer, William Abbott. It has not been sold since. In 1779 a descendant, Paul Orchard, demolished the old house and built a new one in the Gothick style. It faced inland and uphill, with a crenellated parapet and Gothick traceried windows, all in a soft grey stone.

This house was taken in hand in 1845 by another descendant, Sir George Stucley, who commissioned Sir Gilbert Scott to build a new entrance annex and outer hall. It is Sir George's alterations and decoration that give the house its present character. Hartland is a free-spirited Victorian interior, bursting with colour and pride in lineage.

Scott's entrance leads through a large trefoil arch into what is called the Alhambra Corridor, the bold spine of the otherwise modest house. Its vault was decorated by Scott in bright blue and white stencils, vaguely related to the Alhambra. The walls are hung with family portraits and pictures of the house. There is a fine G. F. Watts of a boy with a dog.

'Hartland is a free-spirited Victorian interior, bursting with colour and pride in lineage'

The three principal rooms are the drawing room, billiard room (now a sitting room) and dining room. The drawing room is Scott at his most inventive, ostensibly inspired by his better-known work at the House of Lords. There are elongated linenfold panels and a frieze of Arthurian murals by Alfred Beer. The fireplace and doorways are effusive Jacobean revival, adorned with incised columns.

The old billiard room retains its 18th-century decoration, in pale blue with pretty Gothick curtain pelmets. Sir George Stucley brought the fireplace back from Malta on his yacht, unloading it at Hartland Point. The dining room reverts to Scott, almost a facsimile of the drawing room. The room has an expanding round table at which the present baronet's mother used to eat in solitary splendour beneath the heraldic fireplace.

The rest is clearly a family home. The Georgian Little Dining Room contains a Kneller of an 18th-century Stucley, who saved Stonehenge from being used as a local quarry. The library is Gothick, with a charming ogival overmantel and portraits by Reynolds. In the basement is an exhibition of Hartland life in the 19th and early 20th centuries, mostly from Stucley photographs. They embrace local haymaking and war service with Kitchener at Khartoum. Nothing seems to have escaped the Stucley camera.

Photography at Hartland Abbey

The Stucleys eagerly embraced the new 19th-century art of photography. On display at Hartland are a number of fascinating Victorian and Edwardian photographs, copies of pictures from the family's old scrapbooks and albums, many of which feature Stucley family members themselves. In this picture, taken *c*1890 at Moreton, a family home on the outskirts of Bideford, Sir George is the gentleman on horseback.

Left Sir George Stucley had visited the Alhambra in Granada during a trip to Spain and he was very taken with the Moorish architecture and design at the palace. Back at Hartland Abbey he conceived the idea of the Alhambra corridor, with a vaulted ceiling punctuated by pointed arches. The stencilled designs on the ceiling were influenced by the intricate decorative styles seen in the Alhambra.

Killerton house

★★ Georgian house of Devon grandees

6 miles NE of Exeter: National Trust, house open part year, gardens open all year

Below The restrained colour scheme allows the simple elegance of the original front door at Killerton to speak for itself. The half-moon-shaped leaded fanlight is perfectly echoed by the recurring arches in the ceiling.

The Aclands can lay claim to the title of grandest of the Devonian grand, although the guide to Killerton remarks that this was 'sheer genetic luck'. First recorded in North Devon in 1155, their peculiar skill was in producing male heirs when rich heiresses happened to be available. In 1680 Sir Hugh Acland decided to move his chief home to Killerton from neighbouring Columbjohn. His son and grandson both married well and, by the end of the 18th century, Acland land straddled the county from the Exe Valley over Exmoor to Holnicote. This included the best stag-hunting country in England, much to the later embarrassment of the National Trust.

Killerton House was Elizabethan, on a rising site overlooking the River Exe, north of Exeter. By the 1770s, something nobler was required. Sir Thomas Acland asked a young gardener, Robert Veitch, to lay out a new park and James Wyatt to design a new house. As often, relations between architect and client became strained and Sir Thomas decided to rebuild his old house, engaging the little known John Johnson for the task. That house remains to this day, having proved adequate even for the Victorian 'Great Sir Thomas', a man whose territorial leadership, reformism and patronage embodied landed gentility and who straddled the Georgian and Victorian eras. He was born in 1787 and died in 1871.

Trouble was soon at hand. Four generations of Aclands were Liberal MPs before Sir Richard Acland converted to socialism between the wars. In 1942, he announced to his appalled family that he intended to sell the entire estate and give the proceeds to the Socialists. After a spectacular row, a compromise was reached and the estate was added to an earlier bequest to the National Trust. There was a gentleman's agreement that stag hunting may continue, an agreement the Trust subsequently broke.

The original Georgian house stood four square to the view but was a modest place, from the outside little more than a rectory. In the 19th and 20th centuries, alterations were made, a bay window here, a rear extension there and a new entrance to one side. But today's exterior, painted a creamy-pink and covered in creeper, looks pleasantly informal.

The interior is equally so, thanks to Acland possessions covering the walls and shelves, including a fine array of family photographs. The rooms are a contrast of Edwardian informality and some surprising Georgian or neo-Georgian grandeur, with high ceilings, scagliola and Ionic screens. The music room has an organ and a piano which visitors are invited to play.

The drawing room is severely classical, much altered in the 1900s. One picture shows Lady Harriet Acland crossing a river during the American Revolution to plead (successfully) for her wounded husband's release.

The library has its shelves arranged in the collegiate style at right angles to the wall. This gives more space for books and admits more light to read them, sign of a working library. The dining room beyond has a fine plaster ceiling into which a 20th-century Acland has inserted medallions of the seasons, ploughing, sowing, hoeing and reaping.

The Edwardian main staircase gave the house some swagger. Killerton is not a great English house but is full of character. The gardens laid out by Robert Veitch are an attraction in themselves.

Right Among the treasures at Kingston House is the marquetry staircase. Different woods have been combined to create a patterned surface of the kind more usually associated with furniture. Six woods were used, each one indigenous to the British Isles: English oak, brown oak, ash, yew, sycamore and holly. The edges of the treads were originally finished with walnut, but most of these have now been replaced with oak.

Kingston house

⭐ Georgian house with marquetry staircase and unique wall-paintings

At Staverton, 2 miles N of Totnes; now a hotel

Visitors must travel up a lane north of Staverton, then along a farm track, then across a farmyard. Suddenly a dignified stone house comes into view with a *piano nobile* above a deep basement. The front door is at the top of a Baroque staircase. The house has a brick-walled garden and meadows to the rear and is isolated and silent, apart from the owner's giant dogs. This is surely Devon's most obscure but gracious bed-and-breakfast.

Left Kingston House is now a hotel and among the accommodation available to guests is the Blue Suite, which has a bathroom lined with 17th-century oak panels and a 15th-century linenfold door. The walls of the passage that lead to this bathroom display some of Kingston's most exciting wall-paintings. A roaring lion lunges across one wall while exotic birds flit across the ceiling.

The downstairs is conventional, with reception rooms round a flag-stoned hall. The drawing room has painted panels with fluted pilasters, and a dove of peace in the ceiling roundel, indication of the Catholicism of the Rowe family, who built the house in 1743. Interest increases with the staircase at the back of the hall, with a dado crowded with fluting and inlaid with precious woods. The stair may have been an import, since it seems oddly small for its void and the join to the upstairs landing is uncomfortable.

Upstairs is Kingston's treasure. The central saloon is said to have been designed as a Catholic chapel, required to be inconspicuous in the mid-18th century. Over the fireplace is a plaster relief of the Flight into Egypt, a favourite Catholic theme. Two roundels of saints flank what would have been the east-facing altar. On the walls, religious murals are now being revealed by the house's owner beneath a thick coating of wall plaster. This could yet prove a complete and undamaged private chapel.

No less remarkable are the murals in the three bedroom suites. These retain their four posters and original closets, some converted into bathrooms. The Blue Room has a closet decorated with lions and rustic scenery, and a bathroom with wood panelling and painted graining.

Kitley house

⭐ Tudor house remodelled in the 1820s by G.S. Repton

At Yealmpton, 6 miles W of Plymouth; now a hotel

The house is chiefly remarkable for the name of its ancestral (and existing) owners, the Polloxfen Bastard family. The Bastards settled in Devon after the Conquest. A Regency Polloxfen (pronounced Poulson) Bastard acquired celebrity and a fortune by eloping with a local heiress, Jane Pownoll, to Gretna Green. He fended off pursuit by hiring every carriage in Devon on the night in question to ensure that they could not be followed.

The sister-in-law of another Polloxfen Bastard, Sarah Martin, wrote *The Comic Adventures of Old Mother Hubbard and her Dog* in the house in 1805. It was based on the housekeeper's downstairs lair and Kitley is therefore the putative home of her celebrated cupboard. Sarah reputedly rejected the hand of the future William IV in marriage. Had she accepted, the story of Kitley would have been very different.

In 1820, Humphry Repton's son, G. S. Repton, was hired to redesign the old Tudor house and grounds. The damming of the Yealm turned a muddy creek into a freshwater lake, with the house on a slope overlooking it. This house was then remodelled in the neo-Tudor style, one of the first such examples in Devon.

Repton's building has a façade of silver-grey granite, radiating a soft pink in sunlight. The roof is crowned with an artless forest of pinnacles and chimneys, two of them Tudor directly above the entrance. Remnants of the old house can be seen in the side basement.

Kitley's interior has two features of note. One is the entrance hall, festooned with mock-baronial heraldic shields and banners. The other is a Georgian staircase, pre-dating Repton's work; it fills the former Great Hall and is grander than the rest of the house.

On the landing is a model of HMS *Apollo*, the ship commanded by Jane Polloxfen Bastard's father. It captured the Spanish galleon that secured her fortune and trip to Gretna Green. The house is now a hotel.

Knightshayes court

★★★ Victorian house by Burges and Crace

At Bolham, 2 miles N of Tiverton; National Trust, open part year

The Heathcoat family were owners of the world's largest lace business, which they moved to Devon after their factory was burned by rioters in Loughborough in 1816. Loyal workers followed them on foot to keep their jobs. A descendant, Sir John Heathcoat Amory, became a local MP and gentleman, enjoying hunting and shooting. He bought the Knightshayes estate outside Tiverton for his horses. He then hired William Burges to build him a new house on the site, on a rise overlooking the Exe Valley.

Why such a man should have hired as architect an opium-addicted bachelor Gothicist, who dressed in medieval costume, is a mystery. Burges declared that all houses he designed were 'mine' and added that rules 'are made only for incapables' and that 'money is only a secondary concern in the production of first-rate works'. It was hardly a philosophy likely to appeal to Heathcoat Amory. Burges began work on the house in 1869. Not until the family returned from a holiday in 1873 to see a volume of 57 pages of drawings of the interior did things start to go wrong. Burges declared that Knightshayes would be a 'medieval fairyland' and hugely expensive, since 'there are no bargains in art'.

Sir John begged to differ. Burges was sacked and the decorator, J. D. Crace, put in his place. The family firm of Crace had worked at Brighton Pavilion (East Sussex), Longleat (Wiltshire) and Knebworth (Hertfordshire), and were considered the most accomplished Victorian craftsmen. By then, the vast structure was already rising on the hill. Knightshayes was thus a marriage of Burges and Crace, the one a genius of design, the other of execution.

Above When the National Trust took over Knightshayes in 1972, much of Burges and Crace's original Victorian decoration had been covered up. Crace's dining room ceiling and walls, for example, were hidden beneath lincrusta wallpaper. Restoration by the Trust revealed the frieze and inscription. **Centre** Few original features remained in the drawing room, but the Trust's work uncovered this Burgess-designed ceiling, embellished with his favourite 'jelly-mould' motifs. **Right** A false ceiling in the morning room was removed to reveal more fine workmanship by Crace.

The house stands aggressively on a bluff. The façade is Burges at his most bold, in red and yellow stone with steep gabled roof and dormers, French Gothic in style. A giant stair tower to the rear was intended by Burges but never completed. The exterior is now softened by creeper and by the celebrated gardens fashioned by Sir John's grandson; he married the inter-war woman golfer, Joyce Wethered, who became a noted horticulturalist. The house passed to the National Trust in 1972.

The house is entered through a porch under a poem carved by Burges's sculptor, Thomas Nicholls: 'God by whose gift this worke I did begin/ Conserve this same from skaith [damage], from shame, from sin'. The plea was in vain. The Great Hall was the only work completed as Burges intended. Mighty beams hover overhead and a fireplace fills the inside wall. A screen supports a minstrels' gallery.

At one end of the Great Hall marble columns guard the staircase, carried on superb corbels depicting kings, masons, knights, animals and birds. Under the staircase is a bookcase covered in painted scenes from Christian and pagan art, by Burne-Jones and others. Beyond is a smoking room, a later addition of Sir Ernest George & Peto. Here visitors may read magazines but not smoke (why on Earth not?). It contains a charming collection of miniature elephants.

The house is a *tour de force* of Crace. His wallpapers and fabrics relieve Burges's heavy-boned proportions. Flowers and butterflies dance along corridors. Walls are hung with family prints. The main enfilade was to have been Burges's masterpiece. In Crace's hand, it remains an impressive Victorian sequence, spoilt only by the National Trust's addiction to light-reducing gloom, unkind to an already dark house.

The morning room is hung with works after van der Weyden and Rembrandt. The library has Crace decorations reminiscent of Brighton Pavilion, with jelly moulds in the ceiling. Burges had wanted this to be even more a riot of colour, his drawing showing a monk in the corner reading a book. At the end of the range is the drawing room, deep red in colour with painted roof beams. On the walls are paintings (or copies) by Turner, Constable and Bonington. If Burges wanted more than this, small wonder the Heathcoat Amorys took fright.

On an autumn day the grounds at Knightshayes are incomparable. Lawns stretch down below the main front, with paved and topiary gardens to one side, including the famous Fox and Hounds hedge. From the surrounding woodland, the 20th-century Sir John fashioned glades, dells and an arboretum. Gardening, he said, was 'eleven months hard work and one month's acute disappointment'.

Above William Burges found inspiration in Arabic architecture, as seen in the gilded mini-vaults that he incorporated into some of his ceiling designs. These concave motifs are known as 'jelly moulds' after their shape.

Newton Abbot: Bradley

⭐ ⭐ ⭐ A medieval manor with notable wall-paintings

At Newton Abbot, 5 miles N of Torquay;
National Trust, open part year

Above In addition to the fleur-de-lys, wall-paintings at Bradley display strong Christian symbols. The 'ihs' is a representation of the first three letters of Jesus' name when written in Greek. This is combined with symbols of Christ's crucifixion, including the scourge with which He was whipped, the hammer and nails, and the sponge soaked in vinegar that He was offered as He neared death.

How fashions change! When the ancient manor of the Yardes outside Newton Abbot was offered for sale in 1841 a new owner was advised to 'distinguish his taste from that of bygone days and ... render it a suitable appendage to the magnificent Woods that adorn it'. He should build a new house and make Bradley a ruin.

The new house was duly built, and later burned down. The old manor was used for farm workers and aunts. But in 1909 it found a saviour in the Egyptologist, Cecil Firth, a remote descendant of the Yardes. His family, now Woolners, occupy Bradley still, infusing the place with casual charm and guarding its every cobweb, crack and woodlouse against a possible visit from the National Trust cleanliness fanatics.

The house sits in a thick valley of trees reaching into the centre of Newton Abbot. It is superbly old. A 13th-century hall was superseded by a 15th-century one built at right angles. A banqueting hall was tacked onto one end and a chapel onto the other. The main façade, apart from some 19th-century castellation, is entirely Gothic, covered in limewashed plaster. Fifteenth-century oriel windows and deep gables enclose a passage across the façade, concealing the Great Hall behind. A tiny medieval cat-hole can be seen beside the entrance.

The interior is unusual among medieval houses in having corridors, adding to the maze-like atmosphere of rooms, alcoves, beams, changing levels and general clutter. The newer

Above On one wall of the Great Hall, high up close to the ceiling, is painted an enormous coat of arms. Only part remains – the original image must have dominated the room. The arms are those of Elizabeth I and their inclusion in the decoration at Bradley made a bold statement about the owner's loyalty to the Queen.

Great Hall is reached past a screens passage and has a lofty roof, giant fireplace composed of slabs of moorstone and, a concession to modernity, a modern bay window facing the back garden. A huge Elizabethan coat of arms, an assertion of loyalty to the Crown in recusant Devon, rises above the dais end of the hall. Below is a portion of a Tudor screen.

Beyond the hall at this point is the old antechapel and chapel. The latter has seen services as a chicken run, storehouse, billiard room and boot-room. It has been restored, sadly without its old wagon roof but with excellent modern bosses designed by Peter Woolner.

Upstairs at Bradley are some remarkable wall-paintings. Beyond the original hall was a Tudor banqueting hall, now divided and with portions of its walls scraped to reveal two generations of mural work. One is of fleur-de-lys, and includes a quincunx. Another is of rich Tudor decoration, now mostly vanished. I sense there is much more here to be discovered.

Nor is this all. The upper part of the early hall was redecorated in the late 17th century with Bradley's only concession to modernity, a riotous naturalistic ceiling reputedly by the Abbot family of Bideford (responsible for the earlier and very different Lanhydrock, see page 32). It is a charming work, with scallop shells in the corners and branches, leaves and flowers dripping free along the coving. The Devon countryside might have been plucked from outside the windows and applied to the walls.

The rooms at Bradley contain nothing of value and everything of use. It is a thoroughly inhabited house. Long may it remain so.

Paignton: Oldway mansion

⭐⭐ An imitation Versailles in a Paignton backstreet

At Paignton, 3 miles S of Torquay;
private house, open all year

Right The extraordinary staircase at Oldway was installed by Isaac Singer's son, Paris. The enormous painting shows Napoleon and Josephine's coronation as Emperor and Empress, which took place on 2nd December, 1804. The original painting by Jacques-Louis David once graced the stairway, but that now hangs in the Louvre and Oldway displays a copy.

Be ready for a shock. Tucked away behind Paignton's high street is the sort of building Catherine the Great might have thrown up for a courtier outside St Petersburg. Across a gravel forecourt and parterre rises a nine-pillared loggia in shimmering white with, beyond it, a blue-grey stucco façade. It was inspired by the Palace of Versailles and looks it.

Paignton's emperor was none other than Isaac Singer, an American of Jewish and Quaker extraction who ran away from home in New York State at the age of twelve. Eventually, he ran all the way to France, but not until after he had developed significant improvements to the fledgling sewing machine and made his fortune. In Paris he married a French girl thirty years his junior, Isabella, whose beauty was so remarkable that she is said to have modelled the Statue of Liberty for its sculptor, Bartoldi.

The Singers settled in England, and the fortune from Isaac's sewing machines continued to grow. Told to move for his health to Devon, he built himself a house which he nicknamed the Wigwam. When he died, in 1875, he left the then staggering sum of around £15 million.

His third son Paris, named after his last wife's home city, eventually inherited and like most sons left huge fortunes, he was fully occupied all his life in spending it. An amateur

Isaac Merritt Singer
1811–1875

Isaac Singer was a larger-than-life character. After learning a trade in machine workshops, he spent several years as an actor and travelling player, making the odd invention along the way, before hitting the jackpot with patented improvements to the sewing machine. He married twice but had five known families and more than 20 children.

architect, he commenced rebuilding the Wigwam in honour of his belief that he was descended from the Bourbons. He borrowed the loggia from the Place de la Concorde, but his most sensational alterations were inside. Where his father had created a theatre, he inserted an imperial staircase modelled on Versailles' Etage de la Reine. A stupendous double flight rises to an enveloping colonnade. The floors and walls are in coloured marble while, above, Paris commissioned a ceiling copied from Lebrun's depiction of Louis XIV as a Roman emperor in the Hall of Mirrors. The artist, a German named Carl Rossner, was sent to erect scaffolding inside the actual hall in Versailles, to make sure he matched the original colours. Rossner went on to paint murals in Buckingham Palace.

The interior is astonishing. Majestic doors are crowned with the Bourbon coat of arms. In pride of place is the upstairs ballroom, another borrowing from the Hall of Mirrors. It is 127ft long with mirrors dripping gilt. Other rooms and corridors are equally grand, with pillars of French oak, Bourbon emblems, inlaid brass trophies and ornamental doors. As a final touch, Paris Singer had outbid the Louvre at a Belgian auction to secure David's masterpiece, *The Coronation of Napoleon and Joséphine*. He placed it on the large wall overlooking the stairs.

After Paris's death, the family let the house as a country club and in 1946 the Singer family sold the David to a delighted Louvre, which sent a private train to transport it safely home. A copy can now be seen on the stairs. The house was bought by the local council. It added tennis courts in the gardens and municipalized the interior fittings. With imagination it could yet be restored to its full Edwardian glory. For the time being, the Bourbon arms rise magnificent over the Mayor's Parlour.

The Elizabethan house

★★ A restored 16th-century town house

32 New Street, Plymouth; museum, open part year

Poor Plymouth. It was badly blitzed in the Second World War and then subjected to slash and burn by its city fathers. The modern visitor will find it a maze of concrete blocks, ill-sited towers and ruthless road schemes. Most of this damage was done by one man, Patrick Abercrombie, in the 1950s. The old Barbican district would, in France or Germany, have had its façades restored or rebuilt. Here new buildings were inserted with no feeling for the texture of the old lanes and alleys.

The cobbled area round New Street still conveys some of the atmosphere of the port from which the *Mayflower* departed for the New World. Most of the houses were demolished in the 20th century but one of the finest, No. 32 dating from 1580, was saved intact in 1929 and has been preserved as a museum.

The exterior displays the Elizabethan love of fenestration, with three storeys of windows above a storage basement. The upper windows rest on carved brackets and have original leading. The interiors are sparsely decorated. A passage leads from front to back of the house, partitioned from the two main ground floor rooms. In one is an old Tudor settle.

The spiral stairs are of treads slotted into a central newel, probably an old ship's mast. Upstairs is a reception and an eating room, suggesting that the ground floor was probably mercantile offices. The rooms are well furnished, the eating room having carved rush chairs. The attic contains two bedrooms, one with a delightful box bed apparently from France.

Below and centre The main reception rooms at the Elizabethan House are on the first floor. The original owners of the house would have conducted their business on the ground floor and then been able to retire to their private rooms above. The drawing room is furnished much as it would have been when the house was first occupied.

The Merchant's house

⭐ An Elizabethan house with a façade overhanging the street

33 St Andrew's Street, Plymouth; museum, open part year

The Merchant's House is not as evocative as the Elizabethan House but has a remarkable façade. The first recorded owner was a sea captain named William Parker in 1608. The front, in an area otherwise blighted with modern buildings, is of four storeys, each one jettied further into the street on bold granite corbels. Above rise two big gables. The windows stretch in continuous bands across the front.

The interior is now a museum of Plymouth history, but the feel of the old house has not been lost. To the rear of the ground floor are the big fireplaces of two generations of kitchen. The stair's pole supports appear original as is the panelling in the first-floor reception room. The second-floor fireplace is a wonderfully robust work, with caryatids holding their breasts in a suggestive fashion.

That said, it seems a pity that somewhere else could not be used for so inappropriate an exhibition as of Victorian schooling and the Blitz. Houses of Plymouth's noblest era are in short supply.

The Prysten house

✦✦ A medieval stone house built round an inner courtyard

Finewell Street, Plymouth; private house, open part year

The house is medieval, probably built between 1490 and 1500 for a London vintner named Thomas Yogge. We know only that he dealt here in port wine. Business must have been good. This is a substantial property built round a central courtyard. The reference to a priest's or 'prysten' house appears a later misnomer, although the building is now used by the church of St Andrew's next door.

The house lies on an incline, with its lower floor leading into the courtyard, where trade would have been done. This is now a restaurant. The upper floors were domestic and, despite heavy-handed restoration, they remain in their original form. Windows and partitions are intact and two spiral stairs survive.

The rooms have been given ecclesiastical names, with little basis for their attribution. The main reception room, benefiting from a fine bay window, is called the Frater Room. A chair in the Bishop's Room was amalgamated by a Victorian carpenter from fragments of church pews. Upstairs is the Grammar Room where the Plymouth Tapestry is on display. This was begun in 1977 and tells the story of Plymouth in more than two million stitches.

The remaining upper chambers would have been bedrooms. They are used for exhibitions and meetings but retain the atmosphere of the old house. Many look down on the courtyard, a precious moment of urban tranquillity.

Left The Prysten House, the second oldest dwelling in Plymouth, is built in limestone with door and window frames made of granite. This studded wooden door is framed by a Tudor arch.

Poltimore house

⭐ A Tudor mansion remodelled in the 18th century, now beginning restoration

At Poltimore, 4 miles NW of Exeter; private house, viewed by arrangement

Poltimore is included here out of expectation. The old house of the Bampfylde family lies in parkland on the outskirts of Exeter, ruined and vulnerable to collapse. At the time of writing, it is in the hands of rescuers determined to convert it into an arts centre. The derelict park is no less precious. The house was a Tudor manor, its surviving ranges round an inner courtyard now encased in Georgian extensions. It was degraded as a wartime hospital and then an old people's home and has not yet recovered.

The front is that of a white stuccoed 18th-century mansion. To the rear is a gabled Tudor range with original windows and a staircase turret in the angle of the courtyard. The Tudor Great Hall was remodelled by the Georgians as a saloon, its walls covered in superb Rococo stucco-work. Much of this survives and is recoverable.

The same may be true of the early-Victorian alterations made when the Bampfyldes were raised to the peerage in 1831. A grand staircase worthy of *Gone with the Wind* was built out into the rear courtyard, facing a new entrance in the 18th-century range. The new owners want to destroy it to create an architecturally fashionable glass wall, utterly out of character with what is a remarkable composition. That such a fine building should have been brought to this pass is a poor comment on the county of Devon.

Left Much of the Rococo plasterwork in Poltimore's saloon remains. This stucco frame, one of a pair set on either side of French windows, once held a mirror. Above each mirror was the head of a child, believed to be that of the Duke of Gloucester, the only one of Queen Anne's 17 children to live beyond infancy; he died in 1700, aged 12. The heads have survived and it is hoped that they will be restored.

Powderham castle

✦ ✦ ✧ Ancient family seat overlooking the River Exe

At Powderham, 6 miles SW of Exeter; private house, open part year

Powderham has been the seat of the Courtenays, Earls of Devon, for six centuries and is proud of it. The guidebook folds out to reveal not a picture of the castle but a monstrous family tree. The house is still the family home and the Earl welcomes the visiting public as themselves 'making a contribution to our heritage'. He is right. This is the only way these great houses will enjoy true security.

Powderham presides over an extensive park on the banks of the River Exe. It was never a castle but a fortified manor, the old structure buried in later additions. The exterior is formed of a picturesque jumble of periods. No sooner

Left The dining hall at Powderham is a thoroughly Victorian room. Built for the 10th Earl, it features coats of arms that trace the history of the Courtenay family.
Right By contrast, James Wyatt's music room is a fine example of a late Georgian interior. The gilt sofas and chairs are copies of the room's original furniture; each arm is supported by a dolphin, the Courtenay family crest. Wyatt's favourite sculptor, Richard Westmacott the Elder, created the marble fireplace surround. The carpet was designed especially for the room by the founder of the Axminster factory, Thomas Whitty.

'It is a family tree in architecture.'

does one guess a patch to be medieval than it appears Georgian, no sooner Georgian than Victorian and no sooner Victorian than medieval. It is a family tree in architecture.

The main front to the courtyard is mostly Victorian and was battlemented by the Exeter architect, Charles Fowler, designer of Covent Garden market in London. The great dining hall, also by Fowler, is aggressively neo-medieval. The fireplace is decked with heraldry in a sort of fairground Gothic, the panelling brilliantly coloured and restored. On the north wall is a family group of 18th-century Courtenays by Thomas Hudson.

The ante-room beyond the hall contains the castle's eccentric treasures, two giant Baroque bookcases made by J. Channon in 1740. They are on dolphin feet and inlaid with brass, crowned with stupendous broken pediments. They were given in lieu of tax to the V&A then restored by the Museum to Powderham on permanent loan, an admirable example of modern conservation finance. Beyond are two Georgian libraries with deep blue wallpaper and bright Rococo ceilings.

A large music room was added by James Wyatt in 1794. This was after the coming-of-age ball of the 3rd Viscount Courtenay, later 9th Earl of Devon, had been held in a marquee – presumably to the family's shame. It has all Wyatt's delicate sophistication. A coffered dome rises above walls of scagliola pilasters. Pipers flank the marble fireplace, above which Greek maidens play and dance. Over the mantelpiece

is the Viscount in his masquerade costume. He looks like a cavalier prince. (His descendants prefer to be depicted in sweaters and corduroy.)

The staircase hall was fashioned in 1736 from the upper end of the medieval Great Hall, clearly a massive chamber. Pevsner eulogizes the staircase as the most spectacular architecture of its date in the West Country. Three flights have three twisted balusters to each tread, with the nobility of a London palace. The stair's character is dominated by its brilliant turquoise colour, on which voluptuous Rococo fronds and trophies are picked out in cream. The plasterwork of *c*1755 is not by an Italian but by a local man, John Jenkins. The portraits seem overwhelmed.

A range of upstairs bedrooms displays the usual family paraphernalia, including a charming rocking-boat. A crimson and gold state bed has a sweeping tent canopy crowned with a viscount's coronet, while a small corridor is lined with Chinese wallpaper and the poles of the last Empress of China's litter. Such things do we find in English houses.

What is left of the old Great Hall survives in Georgianized state, but with three medieval arches still leading to the kitchens. The room contains a magnificent long-case clock, reputedly another work by Channon. The Chapel at Powderham has excellent Tudor pew ends from the old church at South Huish.

Left The staircase hall is dominated by the Rococo plasterwork decoration. This was the work of a local man, John Jenkins, and two assistants from London. The original cost estimate was for £217.8s, equivalent to about £23,000 today, but the final cost came in at £355.14s – around £37,000 in today's money. The stairs themselves were the work of James Garrett of Exeter; the heraldic creatures bearing lamps that sit on the newel posts were added in the 19th century.

Puslinch

★★ An early 18th-century mansion built in Queen Anne style

At Yealmpton, 6 miles W of Plymouth; private house, open for groups by arrangement

Puslinch lies above a creek of the River Yealm opposite Kitley. Although Georgian in date (1720), it is Queen Anne in style, standing proud against the hillside. Boundary walls flank the rear garden, beyond which meadows rise to woods. The house is privately tenanted and beautifully decorated, after having degenerated into a cat and dog home in the 1970s. On my visit the lady of the house was trying to drive a flock of vagrant sheep from the lawn.

The estate belonged to a Plymouth surgeon, James Yonge, who decided to build a new house uphill from his old Tudor property. The style is plainly old-fashioned, a mansard roof with overhanging eaves. Dormer windows have alternating triangular and segmental pediments. Inside the most remarkable feature of the interior is its completeness. The rooms are as they would have been in the 17th century, with a state bedroom on the ground floor and closets adjacent to each bedroom on the first.

The hall is a handsome chamber with tall ceiling and six doors giving access to every ground floor room. Like all the main rooms, it retains Georgian panelling, painted except in the dark oak dining room. Most of the fireplaces are identical and in local marble. The handsome staircase has three balusters to each tread and is dominated by a massive still-life in the style of Frans Snyders.

Puslinch is crammed with paintings and prints collected by the present occupants. I know of few houses so warmed by the presence of art, both ancient and modern. Not an inch, even in closets and lavatories, is unadorned by pictures. Every shelf and mantelpiece is cluttered with sculptures and found objects. Bedrooms are all in use, one with a bed designed by Lutyens. The garden at Puslinch contains one of the largest ginkgo trees in England.

Saltram house

★★★★ Grand mansion with Adam rooms and a 'Chinese Chippendale' suite

3 miles E of Plymouth; National Trust, open part year

After the Second World War, the Parker family, Earls of Morley, found their line reduced to two elderly bachelor brothers. They tried to behave as if nothing had changed and briefly restored Saltram's pre-war complement of a dozen indoor staff. But when one brother died in 1951 and incurred crippling death duties, the other gave up the struggle. House, grounds and contents came to the National Trust.

Such has been the outward spread of Plymouth that Saltram is no longer an adornment of its surrounding countryside, more a desperately precious stretch of park amid the enveloping suburb. Already the A38 has cut through its grounds and plagued them with noise.

The house was originally Tudor, but was afflicted with owners variously venal, extravagant and dedicated. The early proprietors, the Baggs, were thieves and scoundrels. A 17th-century Bagg stole £55,000 given him by the Crown to equip a fleet to attack Cadiz, sending it to sea unprovisioned and leading to the deaths of 4,000 men. The house passed to the Parkers in 1712, their extravagance matched only by their ability, like the Aclands of Killerton, to marry money at the right time.

In 1743, John Parker married well and clad the old Tudor building in a set of Palladian façades. The pediments, pavilions, canted bays, Venetian windows and urns form an amateur but engaging composition, brilliant in white render. But somehow the exterior of Saltram seems no more than a stylish box, a container for the wonders within.

In 1768, Parker proceeded to refurbish the interiors with the help of Robert Adam. They are among Adam's best later works, enhanced by fine pictures from the Parker collection. The house is today regimented by the bossiest team of National Trust wardens I have yet encountered. I thought I would be horsewhipped for retracing my steps.

Above This painted mirror in a gilt Rococo frame is one of many pieces of 18th-century chinoiserie that can be seen in the Mirror Room at Saltram. Chinese art was a popular source of inspiration for European decorative arts in the 1700s and Chinese motifs were used to ornament all manner of objects.

Above The saloon is typical of the tasteful, restrained classicism that marks out interiors by Robert Adam. The furnishings and fittings – including chairs by Chippendale and carpet by Axminster – are perfectly suited to the style, with motifs from classical art and architecture in the decorative details: the legs of the chairs and tables are fluted tapering columns, the side table is ornamented with gilt swags, the candelabrum is supported by an urn.

The first rooms are early Georgian. The entrance hall is encrusted with plasterwork, its chimneypiece carrying a relief of Androcles and the Lion. The ceiling depicts Mercury, the god, among other things, of roads, which seems appropriate at Saltram. The adjacent morning room is hung with pictures three rows deep in 18th-century style. Italian masters are interspersed with Saltram's many excellent Reynoldses. The painter was born in the adjacent parish and often visited the house.

The Velvet Drawing Room predated the Adam rooms but begins an enfilade of which they are part. Gilded Corinthian columns frame the doorway to the saloon. Walls are heavy with Canaletto, Teniers and de Hooch. A scagliola table carries *trompe-l'œil* playing cards.

Adam's saloon was a room with 'no expense being spared'. A Venetian window lights a ceiling of fans fluttering above tropical leaves. An Axminster carpet replies with an echoing pattern. Chippendale's chairs do likewise. Over the mantelpiece hangs an early copy of Titian's *The Andrians*, once owned by Reynolds, its frame by Chippendale. In the adjacent dining room Adam adjusts his decorative programme to a smaller scale, with softly modulated colours.

The spacious staircase hall reverts to Saltram's earlier Georgian period. Its ceiling is a burst of Rococo activity while on the walls is the choice of the Saltram collection: Rubens' *Duke of Mantua*, Stubbs' *The Fall of Phaeton* and works by Angelica Kauffmann, including her portrait of Reynolds. Upstairs is a suite of Chinese Chippendale rooms. One bedroom contains wallpaper depicting scenes from Chinese daily life, said to be the most expensive of the genre. The bed is attributed to Chippendale and the walls carry Chinese painted mirrors in Rococo frames. The dressing room walls have rare 'Long Eliza' wallpapers, much coveted for depicting unusually tall women, a Chinese rarity.

Saltram ends on a pleasantly dying fall with the Georgian living rooms used by the Parkers towards the end of their occupancy. In the library, Reynolds comes not singly but in rows. The Mirror Room beyond is a Saltram favourite, darkly oriental with original wallpaper and painted mirrors, some lacquered, some with gilt Rococo frames. The reflection of the viewer is made to mingle with the work of the Chinese artist, an eerie effect.

Below The plasterwork in the dining room, as in the saloon, was the work of the famous stucco artist, Joseph Rose. In addition to the light, delicate patterns on the cornice and ceiling, plasterwork was used to create frames for pictures by the decorative painter, Antonio Zucchi.

Sand

 A hall house with Elizabethan façade

Near Sidbury, 3 miles N of Sidmouth;
private house and garden, open part year

Above The dining hall at Sand is home to a massive
sideboard. Made in the 19th century it includes this
17th-century panel depicting a crowned man, carrying a
sword and flanked by mythological creatures.

Sand has belonged to the Huyshe family
(pronounced Hoo-ish) since the 16th century.
The land has not been sold since 1584, when it
was bought by a London grocer, James Huyshe,
who had twenty-nine children by two wives.
The old house, clad in roughcast grey stone, has
defied time and economics ever since, clinging to
the edge of a steep valley above the River Sid.

Most unusually, there appear to have been
two hall houses co-existing next to each other
through the Middle Ages. One was detected only
recently, buried within a thatched barn in an
outbuilding. The façade of the main house is late
Elizabethan, completed by Huyshe in 1594.
The front has gables along its roofline and a
two-storey porch. A conventional Great Hall is
flanked on either side by family and service
wings. A later member of the Huyshe family
added a rear extension for more bedrooms and
bathrooms. Apart from restoration after fire
damage, the house is as built.

The screens passage has, looming over it, an
extraordinary find in rural Devon, a huge stuffed
alligator. It is believed to have been brought by
a Baptist Huyshe from America in the 17th
century. The inner side of the Great Hall screen
has Artisan Mannerist motifs, a style repeated in
the dresser on the other side of the room.

An old spiral staircase leads upstairs to the
former Great Chamber, surviving from a pre-
Huyshe house. It has a medieval fireplace with
Gothic quatrefoils. Another staircase, with oak
panelling, serves the old kitchens on the far side
of the hall. This was panelled in the last century
with wonderfully gnarled oak. The garden
contains a thatched 17th-century summer-house
looking out over terraced gardens.

Shute Barton

★★ Medieval mansion with
15th-century Great Hall

2 miles SW of Axminster; National
Trust, open part year

On a fine day, the drive from Axminster to Shute Barton is the essence of rural Devon. The road dives in and out of woods, with sudden views over meadows down to the River Axe. Suddenly round a bend is an old gatehouse, and beyond it a courtyard and range of medieval buildings. The house is tenanted and visits must be accompanied by a National Trust guide. Shute Barton cannot be enjoyed in peace.

The land belonged to the Bonville family, passing to the Poles under the Tudors. They demolished much of the medieval house in the 18th century to build the neighbouring Shute Hall. The old property became a farmhouse, inherited by a branch of the Carew Pole family in 1926 (see Antony House, Cornwall, page 16). They gave it to the National Trust in 1959 but insisted that the family remain as tenants, which they do.

Entry is into the old kitchen with reputedly the largest fireplace in England – a claim so often made that it is surely time to decide. Two oxen can apparently be roasted here at once. Most of the accessible rooms seem more domestic than medieval. The drawing room has 17th-century panelling and numerous Pole portraits. Alcove windows look out over peaceful woodland.

The most remarkable relic is the old Great Hall on the top floor, Elizabethan style, reached by a tiny spiral staircase. So magnificent is its roof as to suggest that the floor may be a later insertion dividing a chamber that once extended to the floor below. The room is *c*1450 and has a garderobe in the corner. It is wonderfully bright, lit by windows on both sides with views over lawns to woods beyond. Here one can truly sense old Devon.

Outside in the courtyard is a tiny walled garden surrounded by what appear to be fragments of the old house.

Sidmouth: Sidholme

⭐ A Regency seaside villa with private chapel

Elysian Fields, Sidmouth; now a hotel

In 1826, the 6th Earl of Buckingham, a clergyman, built a villa for himself and his large family. Then called Richmond Lodge, it sits on a slope above the resort of Sidmouth. The address says it all. Sidmouth was and still is a charming enclave of Victorian villas looking out over wooded glades to red cliffs and the sea.

Buckingham's villa was simple, with a carriageway where now is the entrance hall. It is said that the Countess did not get on well with the local vicar, so the Earl built an extension for use as a private chapel across the carriageway. His wife had a window inserted so that she could see who was coming and going, and this survives inside the present hall. A later owner, the Davidson family, filled in the carriageway and inserted a spectacular staircase and landing.

The main house retains its Regency bargeboards, verandas and spiral stairs, looking over gardens filled with sub-tropic vegetation. Palms mix with azaleas, cedars and sequoias, framing views of the coast below. The best feature of the interior is the Earl's chapel, now a music room for what has become a Methodist holiday hotel. It is in the form of an irregular bow with eight windows lighting a large vaulted roof. Between the windows are Rococo mirrors beneath a star-spangled roof. A splendid organ occupies one wall. The room is still used for concerts.

Tapeley park

★ A 19th-century house built in Georgian-revival style, set in an exotic garden

3 miles NE of Bideford; private house and garden, open part year

The site of Tapeley Park is said to have been spotted from the sea by the telescope of William Clevland in 1702. He declared, 'That is the place for me.' He married a local girl and eventually acquired the property. Few Devon houses have so spectacular an outlook. Below are spread the environs of Bideford. Beyond are the sand bars of Bideford Bay with the island of Lundy and the Atlantic in the distance.

In 1855, the house passed to the Christie family when Augustus Langham Christie married Rosamond, daughter of the Earl of Portsmouth. She claimed descent from no fewer than 149 Garter Knights, 60 men 'executed by their monarch' and 11 canonized saints. Small wonder she found Tapeley 'very plain and rather dreary'. She evicted her husband from the house because of his 'childish behaviour' – allegedly, kicking the furniture with his boot to annoy her – and commissioned the neo-Baroque architect, John Belcher, to redesign the house. Her husband took his revenge by leaving the house to a Canadian cousin and then dying. Rosamond went to court to prove that he must have been insane, and won.

Her son was John Christie, founder of Glyndebourne Opera, who spent half his time in Sussex and half at Tapeley. His daughter, also Rosamond, ran the house until her death in 1988, showing visitors round with a parrot sitting on her head. Her nephew, Hector, is now in charge. The house is to outward appearance a handsome Georgian villa, of brick with stone pilasters and entrance porch. The garden is of tropical lushness. The drive rises past pines and pampas grass to reach the Dairy Lawn. The side elevation of the house is here colonnaded. The main front beyond looks out over the Italian garden, which descends the hillside in a series of spectacular terraces. In the distance is a lake. On a hot summer's day, this might be the Ligurian riviera, with Shelley coming to tea.

'Few **Devon houses** have so **spectacular an outlook.'**

Tiverton castle

★ ★ A medieval castle enclosing later buildings

At Tiverton, 12 miles N of Exeter; private house, open part year

Tiverton Castle is a jolly place, although we might not think so from outside. It is approached past the medieval walls of the old fortress still standing to the north of the church in the centre of the town. Old Tivertonians recall crossing to the other side of the road in front of the house, so forbidding was its exterior.

The castle belonged to the Courtenays, medieval Earls of Devon (see Powderham, page 112), and was built in its present form in the 14th century. The building was rectangular, with four towers defining a courtyard above the gorge of the River Exe. The gatehouse still stands facing the road to the east. The old residential quarters faced the church but these are now ruins. It is said that a network of tunnels runs from them into the town. The castle was held for the Crown in the Civil War but the town was for Parliament, the castle being severely slighted as a result. It passed to the Carews in the 18th century and to the present owners, the Gordons, in the 20th.

Entering the courtyard from the church, the ravine of the Exe is to the left and the surviving medieval and Elizabethan ranges are to the right, hard against the wall. In the middle of the courtyard is a surprise, a pleasant villa built by the family in the 18th century, with the appearance of a country rectory rather than castle mansion. The grouping is picturesque, enhanced by a profusion of wild flowers bursting from every crevice of the old walls.

The public is usually shown only the older ranges, including the 16th and 17th-century chambers displaying armour and historic portraits. The tower offers a good view of Tiverton and the surrounding hills. A lower room was once a surgery for a doctor who occupied the adjacent Gothick cottage outside the wall. The castle was haunted by a ghost with a bad cough. One night the doctor left out a cup of linctus which had vanished the following morning. So had the ghost.

Ugbrooke house

Near Chudleigh, 10 miles S of Exeter; private house and garden, open part year

Ugbrooke looks like an ugly duckling in a gilded nest. The house sits in a beautiful valley over the River Ug, its landscape fashioned by Capability Brown in the 1770s. The visitor is greeted with a grove of gentle oaks and a Spanish garden. The house was an early work by Robert Adam, begun in 1763 for the Catholic Cliffords. Only fragments of his work survive inside while the outside is a rare and not especially attractive Adam exercise in castellar style, with round arched windows and doors. In 1874 the walls were harshened with grey render. The entrance now looks rather like a Territorial Army barracks.

The house has been rescued from near death. The 11th Lord Clifford abandoned it before the Second World War to use as a school and hostel. It degenerated into a semi-derelict grain store, the Adam rooms filled with agricultural equipment and produce. In the 1960s, however, the present Cliffords decided to salvage it for family use, a prodigious and successful undertaking. The interiors are mostly of the 1960s, not a good time for country house restoration, but the task is done.

Adam is now encountered only in the occasional ghostly frieze or doorcase. But the dining room contains a collection of Dutch masters and the chapel wing has an intriguing museum of Catholic objects and relics. As at Coughton Court (Warwickshire) or Stonor (Oxfordshire), one sees at Ugbrooke a house whose faith is reflected not just in a chapel but in generations of devout acquisitions. A portrait of a Clifford cardinal hangs on the stairs. The Cardinal's Bedroom is scarlet-hung, with an ecclesiastical four-poster and lavish reliquary. The Tapestry Bedroom next door has cream wall-hangings, embroidered at each corner as if a picture frame.

The most evident Adam survival is the chapel wing itself, reached through a magnificent semi-circular library in olive and white. The chapel has a rich Victorian apse and family gallery. Next to it are two museum rooms, one of Cliffords ecclesiastical and the other of Cliffords military.

Prior Park

Som

Somerset

Above left This fireplace with its painted overmantel, installed by the Strodes in 1625, is one of the few original features still to be seen inside Barrington. **Above right** The original staircases did not survive Barrington's many years of neglect. Arthur Lyle had these oak stairs built in the 1920s, using reclaimed 17th-century banisters from a Scottish castle.

Barrington court

⭐ ⭐ Great Elizabethan house, restored in the 20th century

At Barrington, 4 miles NE of Ilminster; National Trust, open part year

Many owners destroy houses. Some houses destroy owners. Barrington is one, a monument to Elizabethan *folie de grandeur*. The Earl of Bridgwater spent ten years in the 1550s trying to complete Barrington, and failed. On his death, it is said that there was not even the 'means to buy fire or candles or to bury him'. Modern house owners at the mercy of innovative architects may feel the same. The work was finished by a London merchant, William Clifton, and the house then passed through various hands to the Strode family, who added the 1674 stable block next door.

Nor was that the end of Barrington's travails. It suffered death by a dozen ownerships. By the end of the 19th century, it was little more than a barn, its fittings gone and its windows bricked up. Such a place naturally caught the attention of the eager founders of the National Trust and was bought before the days of caution, and the requirement that all acquisitions should be properly endowed. For years afterwards the cry of 'Remember Barrington' struck terror into the National Trust's treasurers and committees.

Then, in 1920, a literal 'sugar-daddy' appeared. The sugar baron, Colonel Arthur Lyle, leased the house and completed its full restoration. Lyle reclothed its stripped rooms with his collection of historic woodwork. He sent boxes of soil to the elderly, almost blind Gertrude Jekyll, who was able to suggest what would grow by merely crumbling the soil in her fingers.

Above An aerial view of Barrington shows how close to the main house William Strode built his stables in the late 17th century. Barrington itself is built of Ham stone and rises above the roof line of the red-brick stable block. The stables were originally open on their north side, but alterations in the 20th-century enclosed the courtyard to create an impressive home, now Strode House (see overleaf). The series of gardens to the west of Strode were designed by Gertrude Jekyll.

Lyle employed the architect J. E. Forbes to restore Barrington and also its old stables, now Strode House next door (see page 130). He built estate houses in the Arts and Crafts style, producing a medievalist's garden city of cottages, farmhouses and stables spaciously planned and decorated with heraldic beasts. Barrington was occupied by Lyle's son until 1978 and in 1986 sublet by the third Lyle generation to Stuart Interiors as a design and antiques showroom. The house was saved, but not its atmosphere. The interior might be a National Trust supermarket. The furniture is admirable and everywhere, but every piece has its price attached.

The exterior is a Tudor E-plan in Ham stone, its south front crowned by a forest of gables, finials and twisted chimneys. The reverse front is almost as fine but its symmetry is broken by large chimney flues. Downstairs, the Great Hall and parlours are decorated with Lyle's imported collection of linenfold and lozenge panelling. The spiral oak stairs are modern but finely executed in the prevailing Jacobean style. Upstairs, the Grand Chamber has a restored fireplace and overmantel with extensive surviving paintwork. This is not for sale. The four-poster goes for £18,000 and the Elizabethan table for £4,500. Strangest feature is the top floor, a gallery with corridors into the gables covering the entire roof area and completely empty apart from imported panelling. It is like a hotel with no guests. Surely more could be made of this great house.

Barrington: **Strode** house

⭐ 17th-century stables, transformed into a 20th-century home

At Barrington, 4 miles NE of Ilminster; National Trust, open part year

The 1674 stables of Barrington Court were converted by J. E. Forbes as a residence for the Lyles while he was working on the house next door. In doing so he created a Jacobean revival house in its own right, one that must have seemed the more comfortable by far. While Barrington Court sits in lonely commercial splendour, Strode House is busy and friendly.

The redbrick building sits round an arched courtyard that once comprised the stables of the big house. A steep pitched roof is surmounted by neo-Jacobean chimneys. Inside, the courtyard space is well handled, the roof sweeping down past large dormers in the Lutyens style. The interior has an Arts and Crafts staircase which appears to rise in waves rather than steps. The building now contains a National Trust shop but the old morning room with rich dark panelling survives as a dining room. It was imported from a house in the City of London in the early 20th century and is of the finest quality. The carving of the cornice and doorcases is exceptional late 17th-century work.

Outside are classic Jekyll gardens, semi-formal outdoor 'rooms'. The White Garden is said to be a precursor of the one at Sissinghurst Castle (Kent). A faun dances in ecstasy against a backdrop of an old farm wall with oval windows.

BATH

1 Royal Crescent

★★ Grand Bath town house, restored
to former splendour

Royal Crescent, Bath; museum, open part year

The Royal Crescent is one of the finest sweeps of
town architecture in Europe. It forms the climax
to a sequence of 18th-century streets, lanes and vistas
rising up the hillside from the medieval city core. Bath
was the product of the most frivolous commercial
development, thrown up in a hurry to meet an
obsession of the Georgian leisured classes for quack
remedies. It was the Marbella of its day. Fashion
proved customarily fickle and within half a century
Bath's heyday had passed. By the 1830s, sea bathing
at Brighton was dominating the hypochondria market.

The city was promoted by four men of rare
enterprise. Richard Beau Nash became the town's
Master of Ceremonies in 1705 and for forty years
enforced rules by which new money could commune
with old. Ralph Allen was the businessman who
financed the building of terrace upon stately terrace
with material from his local stone quarries, watching
it all from his palace at Prior Park (see page 136).
His architects were the two John Woods, father and
son. The marriage of these talents was astonishing.
As Bath's historian David Gadd puts it, 'here
familiarity breeds only delight'.

The thirty houses of the Royal Crescent are
articulated by a continuous row of 114 Ionic
columns. The elder John Wood visualized it in the
1750s and the younger designed and executed it
from 1767. No.1 was the show house and the first
to be built. Tenants at £140 per annum arrived the
following year, soon to include the Duke of York.
When Bath's decline set in, No.1 became a girls'

Left The Bath Preservation Trust have furnished the kitchen at
No.1 Royal Crescent much as it would have been in the late
18th century. A dog-powered treadmill turns a spit in front of the
stove, which is topped with several kettles. A wooden salt box
hangs to the right of the fireplace, a pair of bellows to the left.

'The Royal Crescent is one of the finest sweeps of town architecture in Europe.'

school in the 1840s and went on to suffer the general decay of the early 20th century. Not until 1968 was it acquired by a benefactor and given to the Bath Preservation Trust, which now runs it.

The house exterior is old-fashioned for its period, with no trace of the surface decoration then being used by the Adam brothers in London. A simple five-bay façade has a strong cornice and balustrade, designed to show the world that this was the best address in town. At the time it would have looked out over fields and grazing cattle.

The interior is simple in plan, intended for temporary rent not extended residence. Despite the Bath diktat that gentlemen should not entertain in rented property but attend the Assembly Rooms, this house was clearly built for entertainment. It has a dining room and study or smoking room on the ground floor, and a withdrawing room for ladies and a principal bedroom on the first floor. Bedrooms for servants and others are upstairs, kitchens and services are in the basement.

Each room has been furnished in contemporary style. The paintings throughout are of the period and admirably chosen. The dining room is laid for dessert, with pineapples and port. The study has contemporary copies of *The Times*, gambling chips and clay pipes on the card table. The upstairs drawing room is laid for tea and biscuits. Its contents include two lovely Chelsea candlesticks and a William Hoare painting of *A Market Woman Asleep at her Fruit Stall*. The principal bedroom was as much for morning levée as for sleeping. On the dressing table is a holder for face patches.

The most memorable room at No. 1 is the kitchen. Despite its pristine state, it is full of incident. Every inch is covered in Georgian cookery paraphernalia, including wax food. The only thing missing is a real dog being chased round the spit treadmill by a live coal – hence the phrase 'dog tired'. On the table is a lengthy account of such cruelty to animals. There is also a candle that can be 'burned at both ends'.

16 Royal Crescent

★ The central house in John Wood's elegant crescent

Royal Crescent, Bath; now a hotel

At No.16 Royal Crescent, Bath's elegance can be lived as well as seen, albeit at a price. In 1997, the central house of the Crescent was acquired by the Cliveden Hotel group and incorporated with No.15 next door. The house was singled out by John Wood only to the extent of pairing its columns.

The result is a *tour de force* of historic building restoration. From the front, the hotel is unadvertised. Access requires braving a courteous but awesome doorman and at least the price of a drink or cup of tea. The bedrooms are not accessible, except by glimpses from outside. They are sumptuously 'themed' to reflect famous occupants. The entrance hall and staircase have black-and-white tiles and the downstairs sitting room is beautifully restored, with a Gainsborough Dupont of George III.

The rear gardens (below), bought from neighbouring houses and thus more extensive than the frontage, are a surprise. The rear walls of the Crescent houses are of scruffy undressed stone, yet the façades of the old coach houses at the bottom of the gardens form a splendid Palladian group, designed to be seen from the rear windows of the Crescent. They are virtually a stage set – the Villa, the Pavilion, the Dower House and the Bath House – used variously as tea-rooms and gyms. This is Bath as Beverley Hills. Beau Nash would have cheered.

Described by Pevsner as a 'vast semi-elliptical palace frontage of thirty houses', the Royal Crescent was conceived by architect John Wood as a uniform whole. The giant Ionic columns that are repeated across the Crescent's façade support a continuous entablature that unifies the individual houses into one building. Viewed from a distance, it is hard to distinguish one house from another. It is only the paired columns of the houses at either end and at No.16, in the centre of the Crescent, that marks them out from the rest.

Herschel house

★ ★ The simple Georgian terrace home of great 18th-century astronomers

19 New King Street, Bath; museum, open part year

William Herschel arrived in Bath in 1766; his twenty-two-year-old sister, Caroline, joined him from their native Hanover in 1772. They sought work as musicians in the newly fashionable town. He became organist at the Octagon Chapel, earning money so as to pursue his other enthusiasm, astronomy. The two pursuits were in constant conflict, with William rushing home from conducting a concert in order to scan the heavens with his new lenses. Caroline, whose devotion to her brother was absolute, would read him novels as he worked and place food in his mouth so as not to slow his movement. She later became an astronomer in her own right.

The Herschels moved to New King Street in 1780 but stayed there only two years. He was offered a stipend (and later a knighthood) by George III. They were able to take a bigger house near Slough, where William made ever bigger telescopes. But it was in Bath in 1781 that he discovered the planet Uranus and in the basement that he manufactured his early lenses. The house today is valuable less for its astronomy than as an example of how lesser mortals lived in Georgian Bath.

The house could hardly be simpler. On the ground floor is a reception room and dining room, the latter with a Rowlandson drawing of an astronomer. The first floor comprises a drawing room and music room, filled with musical instruments of the sort that the Herschels would have played. There are also displays of early scientific instruments. In the basement is the kitchen, still with its old stove, and behind it in place of a pantry is the workshop. Here are the furnace, bellows and lathe where William ground his lenses and turned his telescopes.

The garden has been replanted as in the 18th century, with cypresses, herb garden and a quince orchard. It was from a platform here that Herschel noted Uranus. Never can the contrast of ancient and modern science be so vivid as in the field of astronomy. This is Bath's forerunner of a NASA space station.

Right The doorway off the dining room at 19 New King Street leads into what would have been the drawing room in the Herschels' day. A full-scale replica of William Herschel's seven-foot Newtonian reflecting telescope, made in rosewood and brass, stands by the window. It was with the original that Herschel discovered Uranus.

William and Caroline Herschel

The Herschels were two of ten children born to a family of Hanoverian musicians: William in 1738, Caroline in 1750. Their work in astronomy brought them both rewards – a royal appointment and knighthood for William and an annual salary for Caroline, a recognition of her role that was unusual at the time. After William's death in 1822, Caroline returned to Hanover, dying there in 1848.

Crowe hall

⭐ 18th-century villa with neo-Georgian interiors

Widcombe Hill, Bath; private house, open to groups
by appointment only, gardens open part year

When Crowe Hall was gutted by fire in 1926, all Bath is said to have come to watch. Only the portico and hall were left standing, with two flanking rooms. To add to the excitement, the decapitated body of the cook was found among the ashes.

The pleasant villa sits amid an enjoyable garden across the combe from Prior Park. It dates from the 1770s and was owned by a family of bankers, the Tugwells, throughout the 19th century. They added bow windows and a baronial hall, rebuilding the interior after the 1926 fire. When the house was acquired by Sir Sydney Barratt, father of the present owner, in 1961, he ripped out anything Victorian that remained. He had an aversion to the period and the style, asserting that 'art stopped short on the death of King William IV in 1837'. Baronial fireplaces went to Texas and the panelling anywhere. The interior was re-created in its original 18th-century form, with furniture and pictures to match.

When asked if the house is Georgian, the present owner replies, 'Yes, but the George is George V.' The result today is a stately Bath residence with the furnishings and pictures typical of English genteel taste in the second half of the 20th century. Nothing is spectacular, all is decorous.

The gardens cover ten acres of preciously preserved combe hillside. They begin above the house with an arboretum and meadow, sweeping round to the Hercules Garden. Here a mosaic under the pond has wisely replaced a statue stolen from above it.

Prior park

⁂ Landscaped gardens with Palladian bridge, setting for Ralph Allen's mansion

Ralph Allen Drive, Bath; National Trust gardens, open all year

Prior Park was 'a noble seat which sees all Bath and which was built for all Bath to see'. It was designed by John Wood senior as a country seat for the Cornish entrepreneur and philanthropist, Ralph Allen. The house dominates the hill south of the city, where Allen also had a town house. It sits at the top of the steep defile of Combe Down running down to the River Avon. Allen wished to keep an eye on the booming spa opposite.

Allen began the house in 1734 in part as an advertisement for his Bath stone. He had just failed to win the contract for the Greenwich Hospital, which had gone to Portland, and was determined to recover from the loss. He was indefatigable. Allen started the first postal system so that those taking the waters could keep in touch with home. He pioneered the Avon Canal and built tracks to transport the stone that he loved and wanted the world to use.

Wood's mansion was, to Pevsner, 'in the Grand Manner, the most ambitious and the most complete re-creation of Palladio's villas on English soil'. Yet no dynasty was founded to maintain it. The house became a Catholic school in the 19th century and saw extensive building at each end of its curved colonnade. The west end is dominated by J. J. Scoles's 1844 chapel, built in a less relaxed classical style.

Left Prior Park is all about vistas. Built on the top of a hill, the house commands spectacular views over the landscaped parkland and the city of Bath beyond. Viewed from the valley below, the house becomes the crowning glory of its own magnificent setting. **Right** The Palladian bridge crosses an ornamental lake at the foot of the hill below the house. It stands on a dam which creates a cascade through the central archway of the bridge.

The school is private except for open days and the interior is of little interest, having been often gutted by fire. The façade can be appreciated and the grounds are in the care of the National Trust, with magnificent views over the city. They are being restored to their original form which was by Allen's friend, Alexander Pope. Here he fulfilled his maxim of landscape design, 'let Nature never be forgot ... consult the Genius of the Place'. Yet Pope's contribution, largely the Wilderness immediately beneath the entrance, was formal and contrived. It is the marriage of his work and that of Capability Brown in the 1760s that makes Prior Park so remarkable.

The walk runs anti-clockwise round the park, starting with Pope's Wilderness and Sham Bridge, then crossing the central vista beneath the school. The view both up and down the combe is spectacular. Up lies the house against the sky, set above flights of steps adorned with twisted urns. Down lies Capability Brown's park. It is not so much a sweep as a swoop of green, cascading between thick groves of ornamental trees to two lakes at the bottom.

Crossing one of these lakes is the Palladian Bridge, copied by Richard Jones from Palladio's bridge at Bassano. It is one of three such copies in Britain, the others being at Wilton (Wiltshire) and Stowe (Buckinghamshire), each a beautiful example of landscape architecture. The bridge shimmers white above a spring mist or radiates gold on a summer evening.

Beckford's tower

★ Regency romantic's tower topped with a belvedere

2 miles NW of Bath city centre; museum, open part year

William Beckford, Regency antiquarian, collector and romantic, was obsessed with towers. On his grand estate at Fonthill in Wiltshire, 'England's wealthiest son' commissioned James Wyatt to erect the tallest Gothic tower in England. As he cried 'higher, higher', the masons continued until the stupendous edifice had risen 260ft. Beckford's financial worries led him to sell Fonthill and much of his collection and in 1823 he moved to Bath. He was not a moment too soon. Two years later, the Fonthill tower collapsed and destroyed the house.

In Bath he soon dreamed of a new tower on the hills north of the city to which he could retreat, to read and dream. In 1826, he began work to designs by Henry Goodridge, based on the defensive *torre* of medieval Italy. The tower was to have his mausoleum, library and sanctuary below and a belvedere on top. No sooner was it finished than old Beckford took hold and cried 'higher!' yet again. An exquisite Athenian lantern, covered in gold leaf, was duly added to the top.

After Beckford's death, the tower had a chequered history, mostly as chapel to the adjacent Lansdown cemetery. In 1995 urgent repairs were necessary to prevent collapse and a local trust raised money to save and restore the structure. It is now in part a Landmark Trust holiday let and in part a museum. Beckford's Scarlet Drawing Room and vestibule on the ground floor are restored, the former with deep red and blue walls and hangings, and a painted ceiling in the style of an Italian villa.

Upstairs, a cantilevered spiral stair climbs past the museum rooms to the belvedere, looking out over the Bath downs and north-west to Wales. This has been immaculately reinstated as in Beckford's day, with long curtains and window stools with, outside, a gilded balustrade. The curtains were intended to be thrown aside in a theatrical gesture to reveal the view to guests. The central column has more steps up to the lantern.

Right William Beckford's tower was designed to be the culmination of a mile-long ride through landscaped gardens. Once there, a visitor would have to climb 154 steps to reach the belvedere at the top.

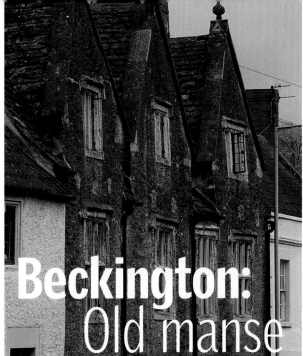

Beckington: Old manse

⭐ Tudor town house behind Jacobean façade

At Beckington, 2 miles N of Frome; private house, open by appointment only

Some houses defy description. The Old Manse in Beckington is a late Elizabethan town house of which Somerset must once have possessed thousands, and now has almost none. What elsewhere would have been of wood and plaster is here of stone. Parts are claimed to go back to 1480, but the three-gabled façade is of *c*1620. The entrance to the house shows signs of having once been wide enough for packhorses, suggesting a merchant's house.

I admire anyone who admits the public to his private house, but there are times when one feels like a voyeur. Amid the clutter are the remains of a fine Jacobean house. The staircase, dividing left and right, has two sets of carved balusters.

The one-time Great Chamber was given a ceiling with strapwork and what appears to be an original Tudor fireplace. Other rooms have mysterious bulges, dips and fragments of plaster moulding. The whole place seems to await a house detective.

The attic, still divided up into tiny rooms as it would have been for most of its life, has a confusion of roof beams darting in all directions.

BRISTOL Blaise house

★ Georgian mansion containing displays of Bristol life, set in a Repton landscape

Henbury Road, Henbury, Bristol; museum, open all year

The village of Henbury is sandwiched between central Bristol and the commercial horrors of Cribbs Causeway. Lost and unsignposted in its midst is Blaise Castle, a fragmentary survival of the Picturesque creation of Humphry Repton and John Nash.

Blaise was a magnet for Bristol visitors in the mid-18th century, when the estate was bought by a sugar merchant, Thomas Farr. He built a fake castle from which he, his guests and tourists could watch merchantmen coming up the river from Avonmouth. The view must have been superb. Farr went bankrupt and the property eventually passed to another tycoon, John Harford, a Quaker and Merchant Venturer.

Harford became instantly unpopular. He restricted access to what had come to be regarded as a public park. He closed footpaths, chopped down trees and demanded back keys which local people had used to reach the castle. He also demolished the old manor and built a square house to express 'substance, directness, dignity and security'. Harford sounds a miserable character.

However, Harford had even more Picturesque ambitions than Farr. He engaged Repton to redesign an entrance away from disagreeable Henbury, and to open up a new view of the Bristol Channel and Wales. Repton's work at Blaise was among his most successful. He was delighted that almost all his effects were achieved 'by the axe', rather than new planting. He used the new drive to the house as an opportunity to give visitors a constantly changing view. 'Where man resides,' he wrote of Blaise, 'nature must be conquered by art.' He later gave way to his partner and eventual rival, John Nash, who designed the eccentric hamlet, built as almshouses in 1810.

Harford's house was typical of the period, solid, simple and unexciting. His son, also John, extended it with the architect Charles Cockerell in 1832 to incorporate a picture gallery. His descendants sold the estate to Bristol Corporation to save it from development in 1926, and Blaise Hamlet passed to the National Trust in 1943. The park is now open and, on a fine day, the castle still offers a view towards Wales.

The house interior is grand, and is now a backdrop to a museum of Bristol life and everyday objects. One room is entirely of washing equipment, another is devoted entirely to lights, and another is a school where Victorian lessons are held. The best room is the old picture gallery, which has pictures from the Corporation's fine collection of mostly Victorian works.

The **Georgian** house

★ Sugar merchant's town house, a fine example of Georgian Bristol life

7 Great George Street, Bristol; museum, open all year

The Georgian House is a simple terraced house just three bays wide, similar to hundreds in the Clifton area of Bristol. It was built for an 18th-century Bristol merchant, John Pinney, in 1788 on his return from making a sugar fortune in Nevis in the West Indies. He died in 1818, worth the equivalent today of £17 million. He was a slave owner and the house contains a didactic exhibition of the West Indian slave trade on the top floor. It was bought by Canon Thorold Cole in 1905, who gave it to the City in 1937.

The house reflects the speculative architecture of this part of Bristol, developed by the Georgian Paty family. The ground floor has been altered to open up the study inside the front door, somewhat spoiling the intimacy of the hall. The room has fine bookcases with broken pediment tops.

On the first floor is the main drawing room. It is laid for tea, beneath Nicholas Pocock's grand picture of the island of Nevis seen from St Kitts. Next door is the library with a magnificent bookcase of Cuban mahogany. Wavy tracery is set into its glass doors. The bedroom above this has a portrait of John Pinney in a colourful waistcoat.

The basement appears to retain its original fittings, including those of the laundry. At the bottom of the stairs is a stone cold-water plunge-bath, which Mr Pinney used as a reminder of his apprentice days in London.

BRISTOL

Kings Weston house

★ ★ Mansion by Sir John Vanbrugh with a terrace overlooking Avonmouth

Kings Weston Lane, Kings Weston, Bristol; private house, open by arrangement

The terrace in front of Kings Weston must have enjoyed one of the great views of England. Below it lay the mouth of the River Avon, through which passed each day a glittering fleet on its way to Bristol, laden with the wealth of the known world. Beyond was the Bristol Channel and Wales. Today, the vista is equally spectacular, but in its ugliness. From horizon to horizon is a sprawl of warehouses, oil depots, car dumps and the M5.

Nor has this majestic house been better treated. It was commissioned in 1710 for Edward Southwell, Clerk to the Privy Council and Secretary of State for Ireland. The architect was none other than Sir John Vanbrugh. He never saw it completed, building continuing for most of the succeeding decade. The house was sold by the Southwells in 1822 to the builders of Avonmouth docks, the Miles family, who sold it in turn in 1937 to the Bristol Municipal Charities. Disaster ensued. The house became a barracks, a school of architecture, then a police training college until, in 1995, Bristol Corporation left it empty to be vandalized. In 2000 it was bought by a valiant private entrepreneur, John Hardy.

The exterior remains glorious, although the grounds are sadly run-down. The main front to the garden has a pilastered portico above which rises an astonishing coronet of chimneys. These are set on an arched arcade running round all four sides of the inner roof, so the chimneys appear to decorate the view of the house from each angle. The chimney pots are paired, offsetting the corner urns. Vanbrugh built this in wood beforehand to see how it would look. It has a wholly theatrical effect and is great fun.

The interior ground floor is accessible and mostly institutional, but no less dramatic. The entrance hall is on a Vanbrughian scale, although altered by Robert Mylne in 1764. An immensely tall space has three decks of portraits in fitted plaster frames, all by 'school of' Kneller and Lely. The second hall behind is equally exhilarating. It is entirely filled by a freestanding 'hanging' staircase rising the full height of the house. On the walls are painted niches and statues. The saloon and other reception rooms have had their plasterwork restored.

BRIST

Portraits of the Southwell family, original owners of Kings Weston, adorn the walls of the towering entrance hall. The paintings hang three rows deep, set in plasterwork frames, and each row has its own style of frame. The grandest stucco work is reserved for the largest pictures in the middle row.

Red lodge

★★ Elizabethan town house with
fine wood carving

Park Row, Bristol; museum, open all year

The desecration of Bristol by its post-war council has outstripped anything inflicted by Hitler's bombs. Park Row is no exception. What should be a stately progress along the contour overlooking the centre is a straggle of unkempt public buildings and multi-storey car parks. Yet in its midst sits a jewel. Red Lodge was built by Sir John Younge *c*1590 as an outpost of his principal mansion lower down the hill where he entertained Elizabeth I on a visit in 1574. If this smaller house is any guide, the big one must have been truly magnificent.

Red Lodge is a fine example of an Elizabethan town house, indicating the wealth and style of Bristol's merchant class. While the exterior has no pretensions, the oak-panelled rooms have some of the best fittings of their period. The Great Oak Room upstairs is the main reception room. It is hard to exaggerate the splendour of this chamber, a match for similar work in the City of London lost in the Great Fire. Decoration is concentrated in the ceiling, chimneypiece and carved wooden porch.

The room's internal draught porch, a fitting all but vanished from most English houses, here serves as a ceremonial foyer. A visitor would have stood momentarily under its arch, crowned by a Renaissance canopy with entablature rising double the height of the arch. It is covered in relief carvings, including Red Indians. The room's classical chimneypiece of stone is no less ornate, its coat of arms puffing out its chest in pride. Local Friends of Red Lodge have supplied some furniture and fabrics. The room is at its best when sun streams through its windows and brings its oak to life.

The other rooms are more conventional. The Small Oak Room next door leads into a bedroom, with good reproduction bed-hangings. The remainder of Red Lodge was much altered in the 18th century. A scattering of pictures and furniture from Bristol's municipal collection can be found throughout the house.

The garden has been laid out as a 16th-century knot garden, using plants known to have been common at that time. It is a lovely parterre, kept in good repair. However, it is a pity about the surroundings.

Right One of the most remarkable features of the Great Oak Room is the ornate draught porch. The tympanum above the door has been carved to resemble a shell. Paired composite columns frame the door and support an entablature decorated with foliage and winged beasts.

Claverton manor

⭐ Regency mansion, now home to a collection of Americana

2 miles SE of Bath city centre; museum, open part year

Below French-influenced decorative style was popular in New Orleans before the American Civil War. A typical bedroom from a Louisiana plantation house of this era has been re-created at Claverton Manor, complete with a Louis-XV-inspired carved mahogany half-tester bed.

Claverton now houses the American Museum and its interior has been wholly converted to that purpose. It was built by Sir Jeffry Wyatville in 1820 for John Vivian in a severely classical style. The entrance is to the courtyard at the back, while two large Regency bow windows face the view on the other side. The façade to the garden is refined Palladian. This was the most elegant period of Georgian architecture, if a little dull.

The museum was opened in 1961 by two American enthusiasts for Anglo-American cultural relations, Dallas Pratt and John Judkyn. All of the rooms have been transported from America, yet this fact is often hard to believe, given the stylistic proximity of the two sides of the Atlantic in the 18th and 19th centuries. The Jacobean Keeping Room, the Lee Room, the Deming Parlor and Conkey's Tavern might all be from southern England. Only the portraiture is clearly 'colonial'. The most evidently American rooms are the Shaker and Mexican Indian ones. The New Orleans Bedroom, heavily classical in style, is betrayed only by its mosquito net.

The grounds are outstanding, with a colonial herb garden and a section copied from Mount Vernon outside Washington. The original had itself been planted with seeds (and even a gardener) sent from Bath. It has thus come home.

Cleeve abbey

⭐ Surviving residential ranges of a Cistercian monastery

Near Washford, 3 miles SW of Watchet; English Heritage, open part year

Cleeve Abbey sits in a valley below the Quantocks in traditional Cistercian isolation. The abbey was prosperous before the Dissolution, after which its church was demolished. Some residential buildings survived round the old cloister. Used as a residence, Cleeve became a collection of farm buildings in the 18th century and by the 19th was owned by the Luttrells of Dunster.

The enterprising Luttrells appreciated the tourist potential of Cleeve's ruins, not least to bring customers to their Taunton–Minehead railway. The farmer's daughter, Cleeva Clapp, named after the abbey, acted as guide for a shilling a head (a large sum in those days). Her stories of her private night-time 'communings' with the ghosts of monks became hugely popular. The sale of the Luttrell estate in 1949 brought Cleeve to the Ministry of Works, now English Heritage.

The Ministry turned what had been a romantic ruin into what at first looks like a lawn catalogue. Trees, shrubs, creeper and weeds were removed. Aggressive new roofs and floors were inserted, walls turned a dazzling white and stonework scrubbed. Cleeve might come from a build-your-own-abbey kit. Any remaining patina of age was lost.

Entry is through an outstanding medieval gatehouse at some distance from the site. Ahead is the old farmhouse, divided into cottages during the Luttrell ownership. It was once occupied by a Captain Angelo of the Indian Army, who grew giant Himalayan tomatoes here. The two surviving ranges of the monastery lie behind, containing the abbot's lodgings, refectory and dormitory.

The refectory is a fine relic of domestic monastery architecture. It has a Perpendicular wooden roof and panel tracery in large windows. The roof has angel corbels and excellent wood bosses. Adjacent are assumed to be the prior's chambers, including a room with painted walls. A large mural depicts a man crossing a bridge surrounded by emblems of the Passion.

At a right angle to the refectory is the most impressive dormitory, in which some three dozen monks would have slept. A door at the far end led to the night stairs into the church. The roof is post-Reformation. Beneath the dormitory are the living and working rooms of the monastery. These include the chapter house and the warming room, where a fire was kept lit throughout the winter. There are Early English windows at one end.

All the rooms are unfurnished. If the English Heritage ideologues can give us, at considerable expense, their idea of a medieval roof, floor and door, not to mention signs galore, why not put in medieval furniture and fittings?

Above Cleeve's refectory is in the southern range of monastic buildings. Some 52ft long and 22ft wide (16 x 7m), it has nine Perpendicular windows with original mullions and tracery intact. The beams of the walnut-wood roof are supported by corbels carved into angels (**below right**) and ornamented with carved bosses (**left**). The tiles from the floor of the original 13th-century refectory are decorated with heraldic devices; here, the arms of Henry III (**centre**).

Clevedon court

✦ ✦ Medieval house with 13th-century defensive tower

At Clevedon, 10 miles W of Bristol; National Trust, open part year

Clevedon Court sits on a series of terraces on the edge of the downs west of Bristol. The scene, wrote John Betjeman, is 'like the background of a Flemish stained-glass window. The Bristol Channel is a bronze shield streaked with sunlight.' Since 1709 it has been the home of the Elton family, one-time wealthy Bristol merchants, now tenants of the National Trust.

The Eltons have been baronets, radical MPs, poets, firemen and potters. Tennyson, Thackeray and John Betjeman were visitors to the house and mentioned it in their writings. Vividly coloured Elton Ware has been sold at Tiffanys. The house contains an Elton collection of glass walking sticks, birds and pipes, as well as prints of bridges and piers. It is a memorial to all these family activities.

Although Clevedon is noisily close to the M5, the main façade retains its ancient dignity. The entrance is a two-storey porch with the Great Hall to its left and a bold chapel window where the dais bay would normally be. To the right lies a curious structure, a semi-detached hall lying at an angle to the main house. This appears to be an earlier hall or barn, backed by a 13th-century defensive pele tower.

This combination of pele and hall is usual in the much-raided Border country of the North but not in peaceful Somerset. Such a tower is remarkable attached to any house in southern England. It is of four storeys with immensely thick walls and slit windows, apparently mid-13th century in origin. Perhaps the early residents considered themselves too close to Wales. The hall is a museum room, filled with Elton Ware.

The main house, built in 1320 by Sir John de Clevedon, thus appears to have been planned at an angle to an older one, perhaps to

face out towards the moor or perhaps to orient his chapel. The latter has bold reticulated tracery in both front and east windows which are incongruously big, as if the mason could only do them church-sized. The solar wing was gutted by fire in 1882, rebuilt and then half demolished in the 20th century. Its side façade was competently reconstructed in a neo-Jacobean style.

The interior was much altered by the Eltons in the 18th century. The medieval screens passage remains, with an impressive row of arches to the service rooms to the right. The Great Hall is now Georgian, with a minstrels' gallery, a Gothic arch to the chapel alcove and, as a surprise, an Elizabethan Mannerist doorway imported from elsewhere. The room is forested with tall-backed Stuart chairs. Portraits of Eltons gaze down from the walls.

The staircase landing is hung with prints of engineering projects and a Tillemans of Clevedon prior to its Georgian alteration. The upstairs rooms are post-fire replacements, except for the chapel. This is a lovely chamber with space only for the family and priest. The tracery is overpowering, enhanced by Clayton & Bell glass which, on a sunny day, fills it with a kaleidoscope of colour.

Cothay manor

★★★★☆ A medieval manor house, complete with gatehouse

4 miles W of Wellington; private house and gardens, open part year

In the grounds of Cothay Manor are avenues down which medieval ladies would exercise their unicorns. Since these beasts, as we know, were visible only to virgins, it was never easy to police this facility. The house was built in the 1480s, 'modern' enough to avoid Tudor alteration yet now incomparably antique. The site was that of a 12th-century hall house, and the owners were the Blewitt family. It was transferred to the Every family a century later and remained an obscure farmhouse until 1925, when it met its saint.

Colonel Reggie Cooper was a bachelor diplomat in the *Country Life* circle of Edward Hudson and Christopher Hussey. Cooper had been at the Istanbul embassy in 1914 with Harold Nicolson (of Sissinghurst Castle, Kent) and Gerald Wellesley (of Stratfield Saye House, Hampshire), all friends of Hussey. In the distant south, they dreamed of English manors, of old stone, rich wood, grey-green tapestries and flickering candles. Cooper had already restored Cold Ashton north of Bath in such a spirit. To Hussey, he was little short of a genius, for whose 'lightness of healing touch ... no praise is too high'. Cooper lived at Cothay for eleven years. It is now owned by the Robb family.

The house sits beyond its own fish pond, lost in the meadows and woods of the Vale of Taunton. Few houses in England remain so evocatively medieval in appearance. The plan comprises gatehouse, courtyard, porch leading into screens passage and Great Hall. At the dais end are a parlour and solar; at the service end is a gallery with upper guest room and small chapel. Some new panelling was inserted at the end of the Elizabethan period, when a small

Left Cothay's ancient, creeper-clad gatehouse was once castellated. It now leads into this pretty courtyard garden. **Above** The Great Hall is unmistakably medieval. The floor at the north end is lightly raised: this is the dais where the high table would have been placed for the lord of Cothay and his family.

Renaissance dining room was constructed. Otherwise nothing has been altered, apart from a few rooms in a wing added by Cooper for his own use. The group is in a restful pink-brown stone, with steep tiled roofs and complete with original fenestration. Even the gatehouse door is medieval.

The Great Hall has a tall arch-braced roof with minstrels' gallery. On a wall is an indistinct painting of Reynard the Fox. The parlour is panelled in oak stained to look like walnut, above which is a painted frieze. The original spiral staircase leads up to the solar, open to another fine arch-braced roof. A small window looks onto the hall. A charming feature of this room is its decoration by the daughter of the present owner, Arabella Robb, in a style wholly

'Few houses
in England remain so
evocatively medieval ...'

sympathetic to its past. Her design is of plants with stalks and tendrils roaming free, even covering the radiator. Here are cornflowers, carrots, sweet peas, tulips, pears, quinces – exactly what the Middle Ages would have done with this space. This is a magic room, somehow medieval and of today at the same time.

Below one end of the solar and next to the parlour is the old undercroft, now a library. Mrs Robb has decorated this in deep red. With its thick beams covering ceiling and walls, it is a chamber of medieval intimacy. Across the hall is the Everys' later dining room. The ceilings are here plastered with vines. The chimneypiece is wood, carved with caryatids of the four Virtues, first glimmerings of the Elizabethan Renaissance. The curtains are modern but based on medieval designs.

Cothay has not finished with us. At the service end of the hall off the gallery and over the porch is a small oratory. This has a squint from the adjacent bedroom. The gallery may have been where the servants gathered to hear mass in the oratory. The priest's chamber next door is known as the Gold Room. It has a 15th-century fresco of the Madonna and Child, badly restored and now hanging away from its wall. More paintings decorate the guest bedroom next door. One, very primitive, is of the Virgin, possibly at the Annunciation. Another appears to be of a Blewitt. Round the frieze is a scroll, its lettering lost. These are surviving medieval interiors of incomparable value.

Even when the house is not open, the garden may be accessible. It is divided by deep yew walls into private rooms of its own. Its dark green recesses reflect the medievalism of the house. Mrs Robb created the avenues for the aforementioned unicorns.

Cricket house

⭐ A Georgian house of Ham stone by Sir John Soane

At Cricket St Thomas, 4 miles E of Chard; now a hotel

Cricket House is set in a landscape of great loveliness. The drive from the main road leads through trees to curve in front of the house. The land beyond slopes down to a series of lakes before rising again to a distant bank of woods. It is best in the gloaming of a summer evening.

The house was altered for Lord Bridport, previously Admiral Hood, by Sir John Soane in 1786 and 1801. It remained in the family until 1897 when it was sold to the chocolate manufacturer, Francis Fry. A wildlife park was developed on the estate in the 1960s and the house passed in 1998 to Warner Holidays, controversial saviours of many English country houses. The exterior lies low and dignified, in warm Ham stone with a Tuscan porch. Some care has been taken to conceal the ugliness of the hotel beyond, but not enough inside.

How much of Soane's interior survives is hard to discern. Drawings in the Soane archive show a library that bears little relationship to the present one. The staircase, the most remarkable feature of the house, is undeniably Soanian, if not by Soane. It sweeps upwards from the hall before dividing and returning on itself to an upper landing. Most of the principal reception rooms seem unaltered and the house has retained some of its dignity. On the walls is a fine collection of French prints.

Dillington house

A mid-16th-century house with 19th-century Elizabethan-revival remodelling

Near Ilminster, 5 miles N of Chard; education and arts centre, open by arrangement

The house is a miniature Barrington Court (see page 128), but while the latter sits isolated amid open lawns, Dillington is tucked into the hills, closely attended by gardens. Faced with Ham stone, its façade glows in the sun, patched with green and white lichen. Since 1949, the house has been a Somerset County Council study centre, open on occasions and visible from the drive and park.

The house is a traditional mid-16th-century E-plan, the conversion of an earlier hall house. The owner was John Bonvile. The house later passed to the Georgian prime minister, Lord North, and was remodelled by Sir James Pennethorne in neo-Gothic in 1838. Pennethorne was Nash's assistant, academic rather than inspired, who went on to design the Italianate west wing of Somerset House in London. He gave Dillington its present symmetrical appearance. As so often with the Elizabethan revival, it is hard to tell restored from new but this façade is a beautifully modulated work, with porch, wings, gables and chimney in perfect balance. It seems a timeless style, forever English.

The interior is institutional but has panelling similar to that at Barrington. It is said to have been removed from that house, which subsequently had to import some more of its own. The screen opposite the kitchen appears old, but is it original? The rest of the house is Jacobethan.

Dodington hall

⭐ A manor house with Elizabethan Great Hall and Mannerist-style fireplace

At Dodington, 10 miles W of Bridgwater; private house, open part year

How have these places survived? The manor house lies on a rise at a distance from the main road, to form a picturesque group with church, barn and farm buildings. All remain intact, looking out across the fields towards the Severn Estuary and the distant coast of Wales.

The manor of the Dodington family now belongs to Lady Gass of Fairfield (see page 160) and is tenanted. It is divided into two houses on either side of the screens passage. The left-hand one is a Victorian re-creation. The right-hand one (painted white) comprises the old Great Hall, apparently Elizabethan, with bay window and solar wing, occupied by an enthusiast for its architecture. The entrance porch has a shell shrine in its wall.

The hall still has its minstrels' gallery and is open to the roof. This displays an extraordinary pattern of scissor wind-braces, while the main beams are cut wavy rather than straight. They rest on angel corbels. It is all restless and decorative, sign of someone having both money and a sense of style. Equally extraordinary is the fireplace. This is of 1581, in an Elizabethan Mannerist style. It is decorated with negroes, Aztec warriors and primitive figurines with prominent genitalia, demonstrating a fascination with the New World typical of the late 16th century.

The arch to the bay window appears Norman, while the window chamber itself has a massively beamed roof. These features cannot be in their original positions. The parlour is again handsomely decorated, with close-laid beams and a 17th-century frieze. The plaster everywhere makes copious use of the Dodington arms of three bugle horns.

Dunster castle

★★☆ Medieval castle with Elizabethan, Jacobean and Victorian additions and adaptations

At Dunster, 3 miles SE of Minehead; National Trust, castle open part year, grounds all year

Dunster is a dream of Camelot. Few castles have a finer aspect. The view from the coast road shows the battlements prominent against the backdrop of Exmoor. A watch tower guards the settlement from neighbouring Conyger Hill. Beneath lies the picturesque village high street.

The castle hill – or tor – was chosen by the Norman lords of Devon, the Mohuns, for their stronghold. It was sold in 1376 to the Luttrells, who held it against all-comers except Cromwell. A Luttrell built the mighty gatehouse, another commissioned William Arnold to expand an earlier house within the walls in 1617. Another refurnished it after slighting in the Civil War and another commissioned Anthony Salvin in 1868 to 'refortify' the castle that we see today. Dunster is like Arundel (Sussex), Belvoir (Leicestershire) and Windsor (Berkshire), essentially a Victorian ideal of what a great medieval palace should be. The castle was only conquered by the taxman in 1976, passing to the National Trust with the family as tenants.

The military prowess of the site is immediately apparent in the steep climb up to the entrance. This has too much distressing tarmac. The north façade is by Salvin, embracing medieval, 17th-century and Victorian elements. The red Somerset sandstone is combined with honeyed limestone to create a pleasing variety of tones. This mix is more pronounced above the terrace to the rear, where walls that would once have seemed unassailable are now picturesque.

The building has two halls, an outer one created by Salvin and an inner one dating from the Elizabethan house. The outer hall is Jacobean revival, taking the place of the former parlour and filling the width of the castle. It is hung with family portraits. The inner hall has a Salvin fireplace

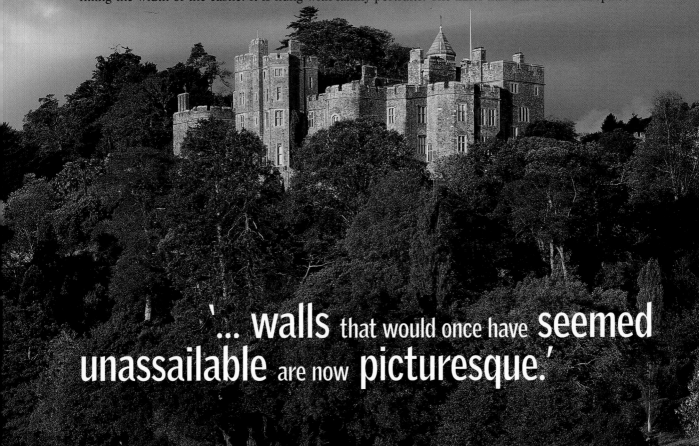

'... **walls** that would once have **seemed** unassailable are now **picturesque**.'

Above left The outer hall is one of Dunster Castle's 19th-century additions. The architect, Salvin, created a Jacobean-style hall, complete with plasterwork ceiling. **Above right** The allegorical portrait of Sir John Luttrell hangs in the inner hall. Luttrell distinguished himself on military service in Scotland but was captured in 1550 and held for ransom by the Scots.

and the iconographical Luttrell portrait of 1550. This extraordinary picture shows Sir John Luttrell, Elizabethan commander in Scotland, rising from the waves, encumbered with allegory. Peace caresses his fist and Venus calms War, while girls hold money bags to indicate the ransom that was needed to rescue him. This is a contemporary copy of the original in the Courtauld Gallery in London.

Beyond the inner hall is the dining room with a fine 1680s ceiling of deeply undercut plasterwork and dark panelling. Of the same period is the Restoration staircase. It displays acanthus decoration running riot over ceiling and balustrade panels alike. Each balustrade is carved from planks of elm, nine inches thick. Hounds dart between the leaves in pursuit of the fox, while Luttrell military trophies adorn the gallery above.

The staircase leads into the much-altered morning room and a sequence of Salvin bedrooms. The downstairs at Dunster was planned for the men, the upstairs for women. The principal bathroom of the 1880s was reputedly the first in Somerset – and the only one in the house. The gallery is notable for its embossed leather wall panels depicting Antony and Cleopatra. These are French or Flemish, of the mid-17th century. Antony is said to look suspiciously like Louis XIII while Cleopatra on her horse appears bemused. The scenes are formal and stylized, especially the deaths of the two heroes.

The King Charles Room was supposedly used by the king as a young prince during his visit to drum up support in the West Country during the Civil War. Its fine overmantel portrays the Judgement of Paris of 1620. Downstairs, the billiard room and library, both by Salvin, complete the male domains. He also built a completely new tower on the site of a former chapel. The view from here out towards the Bristol Channel is spectacular.

The outside terrace that runs across the south front enjoys the same view. The garden steps down the side of the tor in paths lined with shrubs of tropical fecundity. These slopes are sheltered from the north and east winds and bathe only in Channel breezes. Dunster seems to ride on a wave of perpetual greenery.

This magnificent carved elm staircase was installed at Dunster during the Restoration period by Colonel Francis Luttrell. The castle had escaped destruction during the Civil War, despite being used as a garrison by both sides. Seized first by Royalists and then by Parliamentarians, only the castle's defences suffered any real damage. The Luttrells regained control of their family seat at the end of the war, and a few years later began their improvements.

Fairfield

✦ ✦ An Elizabethan mansion with Georgian additions and medieval remains

Near Stogursey, 10 miles NW of Bridgwater; private house, open part year

Fairfield needs a saint as owner and fortunately has one. Large, rambling and with rooms galore, it has lived as many lives as it has seen changes in its family name. The house has remained in the same line of descent since the Middle Ages, variously as Verneys, Palmers, Aclands, Acland-Hoods and the Gass family. The present incumbent, Lady Elizabeth Acland Hood Gass, has both restored the house and revealed much of its past in her uncovering of its walls.

The entrance façade to the drive is restrained and apparently Georgian. This is merely a side elevation of an Elizabethan E-plan mansion, immediately visible round the corner. Here is a most enjoyable façade, with three-storey porch and canted windows to its wings. The date over the porch is 1589. But this is not all. Round another corner are found the remains of an even earlier medieval house fashioned into the left-hand wing of the E-plan building. Its traces are visible in the walls. Fairfield has thus had three distinct façades demonstrating various stages of its history, medieval, Elizabethan and Georgian.

The interior of the house was Georgianized in appearance, if not in plan. The faded walls of the Great Hall are hung with ancestors, apparently in chronological order. The old parlour beyond formed the Georgian entrance hall. The dining room displays various portraits of nautical Hoods, one of whom sailed round the world with Captain Cook in 1772 at the age of fourteen.

An earlier ancestor, Thomas Palmer, sailed with Drake and Hawkins. He produced a son, William, who 'being a person of great learning chose always to live in London'. Early monarchs were keen to keep aristocrats and landed gentry away from the temptations of the capital and remain looking after their country estates. Palmer was duly fined £1000 by the Star Chamber of Charles I for having been so disobedient to the King's demand 'requiring all persons of estate to reside and keep hospitality at their houses'.

Gatcombe court

★★ ☆ Ancient manor with Roman well

Near Long Ashton, 5 miles SW of Bristol; private house and gardens, open for groups by appointment only

'Do you speak house?' I was once asked when visiting an old building, as if such concepts could only be discussed in a private language. Gatcombe Court is such a place. Nothing is regular, nothing of the same period, yet everything pleasing. Owned by the Clarke family, the house is too small to be regularly open, yet the brochure offers appointments for groups, 'hospitality and cost to be cheerfully agreed'. They are best made during the rose season, a Gatcombe speciality.

The house was built in the Middle Ages on the remains of a Roman settlement, evident in a huge rampart in the grounds. This is claimed to be wider than Hadrian's Wall. There is also a floodlit Roman well outside the kitchen. The oldest part of the house survives from the 13th century. To this was added a solar and possibly a Great Chamber above the hall. The left side of the façade has two gables and dates from an extensive rebuilding in 1683. There is a fine staircase inside of this period, rising from basement to attic.

Gatcombe was tenanted until the 1920s and has been steadily restored ever since. Bricked-up windows have emerged under restoration and the outside displays 16th and 17th-century fenestration. The interior is that of a comfortable family home, its walls a fascinating museum of architectural clutter. There is an intriguing lintel, a re-sited chimneypiece, a medieval arch and a series of strange wall holes. The Clarkes have filled every inch with family memorabilia, fusing house and family in a single personality worth a hundred museums.

From the windows can be seen a voluptuous yew hedge and Queen Anne gates – and the illustrious roses.

Above The beginnings of Gatcombe Court were built in around 1254, on the site of a Roman settlement. It then grew, over the centuries, into a typical Somerset manor house. Although a building of historical importance, Gatcombe remains very much a family home, furnished with personal items and hung with family portraits.

Gaulden manor

✦✦ Medieval house with extraordinary 17th-century plasterwork

At Tolland, 9 miles NW of Taunton; private house, open by appointment, gardens open part year

From a lane beneath overhanging beeches a track turns into an old courtyard. On the right is a jumble of medieval buildings that have long made their peace with nature. The house lies ahead, guarded by a two-storey porch and old casement windows. Gaulden Manor goes back to the 12th century, when it passed to the Priory of Taunton.

After the Dissolution Gaulden's owners and tenants came and went. It may have offered refuge to the Roman Catholic Bishop of Exeter, James Turberville, after his release from the Tower in 1563. The Wolcott family bought the house in 1618. They then emigrated to America, thus assuring the house a flock of transatlantic adherents, including a Society of the Descendants of Henry Wolcott. In 1639 the Turbervilles returned and gave the hall its astonishing plasterwork. Since then the house has been a farm, occupied since 1966 by Mr and Mrs James Starkie.

Gaulden is a classic Somerset manor. Dogs yap, fires burn and books tumble from shelves. Mrs Starkie has long been a mistress of the art of paint, rightly divining that the way to enliven a medieval interior is with bright colours, not whitewash. If only the National Trust had her courage. Thus the entrance passage is green. The old kitchen, now dining room, is red. Its fireplace still has alcoves for bread and salt and a herringbone fire-back.

Across the screens passage is the hall, in vivid blue, a room that may once have been a kitchen. Yet it has a ceiling worthy of a great house, its plasterwork dated to the 1640s. This ceiling dominates what is a modestly proportioned chamber. It has a giant central pendant and roundels on either side. One is of the Last Trump, an angel summoning a skeleton, and the other of King David's harp. Round the frieze, some of it like dripping icing sugar, are biblical themes alleged to relate to the saintly life of the episcopal Turberville. The ceiling continues into an alcove known as the chapel, clearly of the same period. The ceiling would seem an act of homage to the ancestral bishop.

A surprisingly spacious double flight of stairs, hung with crimson William Morris wallpaper, leads to the landing and the Turberville bedroom. This has more fine plasterwork over the fireplace from the same hand as downstairs. Everywhere in the house are old prints and pictures of horses and families. In the garden is a medieval stewpond. The old house can be seen from every angle, sprouting from its enveloping greenery.

The Tree of Life

In the grounds at Gaulden is this oak post, carved by a Second-World-War German prisoner who worked on the manor's farm. Known as the 'Tree of Life' it is covered with carved figures that spiral around the post. Each figure represents a stage in a man's life. The story begins with a baby, at the bottom, and is followed by figures that show a man becoming a successful blacksmith, a mayor, and finally, an old, bearded man.

Above When the floor of the dining room at Gaulden was being excavated a well was found in one corner, dating, no doubt, from when the room was a kitchen. **Below** The Great Hall was once open to the roof before the ceiling, with its remarkable plasterwork, was installed in the 17th century. A 16th-century oak screen to the right of the fireplace separates off the chapel.

Glastonbury: The Abbot's kitchen

⭐ Surviving kitchen of a medieval Abbot's house

Magdalene Street, Glastonbury; museum, open all year

Modern Glastonbury is one of the oddest places in England. It is part market town and part fantasy capital of Avalonia. In the latter role it is the pilgrimage centre for Holy Grail searchers, druids, Arthurians, mystics, hippies and drop-outs.

The bush in the churchyard allegedly sprouted from the Crown of Thorns brought by Joseph of Arimathaea. On the great tor, visible across the Somerset Levels for miles round, any legend you care to name is buried. The main street is filled with the odours of herbs, spices and incense. Goodness knows what the monks would have made of this.

I expect the answer is that, as today, what would have been made is money. Glastonbury was founded on an island in the Somerset Levels by Saxon missionaries in the 8th century. Rebuilt by the Normans it became one of the wealthiest foundations in England. Of its monastic splendour little remains but what does remain is outstanding, the gatehouse and one of the best-known works of domestic architecture in England, the Glastonbury Abbot's Kitchen in all its medieval splendour.

Most abbey structures were used as quarries after the Dissolution, but the kitchen survived probably because it was small and therefore useful: it has been a Quaker meeting house and a cowshed in its time. The building is intact, dating from the mid-14th century, four-square in plan and comparable today only with the kitchens at Oxfordshire's Stanton

Harcourt and Berkeley Castle (Gloucestershire).

Each corner contained a fireplace, turned by the masons to architectural effect by making the upper section octagonal, with two tiers of lantern. The smoke would have escaped through chimneys at the corners, other fumes through the lanterns.

The exterior is ornamented, with Gothic windows above the doorway. The lanterns are treated as if they were the turrets of a church, with three sloping roofs interspersed with battlemented panels and windows. This is a beautiful structure, evidence of the prosperity of the house to which it was attached.

Left In 14th-century England, Glastonbury was second only to Westminster Abbey in terms of wealth. The abbot of Glastonbury was, therefore, a powerful man who needed accommodation suited to his position. In 1334, Abbot John de Breynton began the building of new living quarters and the kitchen was part of this programme. It survives today, alongside the ruins of the once magnificent abbey church.

Hestercombe house

★ Queen-Anne house, hidden by Victorian additions, garden by Lutyens and Jekyll

4 miles NE of Taunton; Council property, open by arrangement, gardens open all year

Hestercombe House is no obvious beauty. I was shown round by a custodian who wished it gone. Yet the building is focus of a superb landscape and if its present occupants, the Somerset Fire Brigade (and its chief officer), move out, a more dignified use may be found for it.

The house was that of the Warre family from the 14th century to the end of the 19th (as Warre Bampfyldes). They built the Queen Anne house that lies hidden within the present pile and began landscaping the grounds in the 18th century.

In 1873 the house was bought by Viscount Portman, owner of much of Marylebone and father of the builder of Bryanston (Dorset). His grandson, Edward Portman, in 1904 commissioned Edwin Lutyens and Gertrude Jekyll to produce a dramatic garden landscape on the terraces below the house and up the slopes of the Quantocks behind.

The interior is institutional. Apart from a fine hall and staircase the chief interest is said to be the Chief Fireman's bathroom. The exterior is at best eccentric. The symmetry of the old house was thrown off balance by the erection of a crude Victorian tower to its left. The side front onto the garden has lost all coherence and is just a sequence of bays with a jumble of pediments, windows and recesses in soft pink stone.

The gardens are sensational. The landscape garden runs uphill of the house; this was first designed by Coplestone Warre Bampfylde who inherited in 1750. The garden below the house is by Lutyens and Jekyll, with architecture here in the ascendant. Lutyens's Orangery in Ham stone is a most accomplished work of 'Wrenaissance'.

'The gardens are sensational.'

Lytes Cary manor

★ ★ Medieval manor house, remodelled by Tudors, Elizabethans and Georgians

4 miles NE of Ilchester; National Trust, open part year

The composition of Lytes Cary is delightfully eccentric. The core of the building is a Great Hall with parlours, chapel and Great Chamber to the left of the porch. In front is a garden party of squat yews, like ladies-in-waiting in farthingales. To the right looms a Georgian extension, wholly out of place, an uninvited guest at this medieval occasion.

The original hall house was built by Thomas Lyte in the 1450s and 'modernized' by John Lyte in the 1530s. His son in turn, Henry, was a noted Elizabethan botanist who developed the garden and filled the house with family heraldry. Lytes Cary was a farm until acquired by Sir Walter Jenner, brother of William Jenner of Avebury Manor (Wiltshire), in 1907. Like Reggie Cooper at Cothay (see page 150) and others of the *Country Life* circle, he was an enthusiast for manorial architecture and restored and passed the house to the National Trust in 1949.

The Great Hall is open to the roof, its wind-braces handsomely cusped. An unusual Gothic arch embraces a small dining area, fashioned in the 1530s from the former dais window bay. One can imagine the family tucked behind the screen while the servants went about their business in the Great Hall outside. Adjacent to it is the 14th-century chapel, showing the close fusion of domestic and religious life in a pre-Reformation manor.

Right At one end of the Great Hall stands the screen, restored in a medieval style by Sir Walter Jenner, who purchased Lytes Cary in 1907. The original roof with its wind braces still survives; each rafter rises from a carved angel bearing a shield.
Above The stained glass panels in the triple-light windows of the Great Hall date from the 16th century. The sample above is clearly dated 1592.

The family rooms added as a rear wing in the 1500s are intact. From the garden they look like a miniature Elizabethan mansion in themselves. A two-storey bay of Elizabethan windows in the centre of the façade lights the Great Parlour and the Great Chamber above. The interiors are deliciously dark and ancient, with windows giving glimpses of the gardens below. The Jenners filled them with furniture chosen not as contemporary with the house but as suitable to its scale and style, a subtle distinction.

The Great Parlour has a mirror framed in early embroidery, known as stumpwork. The Little Parlour, where Lyte worked on his herbals, has a pretty 18th-century niche with a *trompe-l'œil* shell backing. The Tudor ceiling of the Great Chamber upstairs is decorated with lozenges and the arms of Henry VIII. Dated 1533, it is said to be among the earliest examples of this style in a private house. The door retains its draught-excluding porch, with linenfold panelling.

Relics of the herbal and horticultural endeavours of Henry Lyte are on display. His Tudor garden disappeared and the Jenners restored the grounds on Gertrude Jekyll lines. But one bed is now planted with Lyte's herbs and a copy of his *Niewe Herball* can be seen in the hall.

Martock: Treasurer's house

⭐ Medieval group in shadow of church

At Martock, 5 miles NW of Yeovil; National Trust, open part year

Below Hugh, treasurer of Wells Cathedral and rector of Martock, occupied this house from 1262 and so gave it its name. A subsequent treasurer, John de Langton, who was also Chancellor of England, added the Great Hall in 1293.

The medieval Treasurer of Wells Cathedral was also rector of Martock. He needed a house in which to live when in town and an office in which to collect tithes and do business. Both survive directly opposite Martock church.

The Great Hall has a high timbered roof and ochre walls the colour of powdered Ham stone. This is clearly a noble room, but the absence of a fireplace suggests it was for business purposes. The 14th-century windows have cinquefoil rere-arches (the internal arches above the window niches) and seats fashioned in their sills as if large numbers of people were expected. On the walls are brackets for oil lights.

Adjacent to this hall is what would have been the old residential hall and solar, since divided both horizontally and vertically. Upstairs are fragments of a 13th-century structure, including a wall painting of the Crucifixion.

To the back is the old kitchen. This has a gigantic fireplace made of two slabs of Ham stone, each 6ft long. Here I learned the derivation of 'curfew', the call each evening for fires to be covered (*couvrez les feux*) to reduce the risk of night-time conflagration.

Montacute house

★★★★ Elizabethan house, refurnished and with Jacobean garden

At Montacute, 4 miles W of Yeovil; National Trust, house open part year, gardens all year

Montacute House came to be regarded as the epitome of grand Elizabethan architecture. Its Ham stone is so richly yellow-red as to look as if made of warm embers. The style lacks the originality of Longleat (Wiltshire) or Hardwick Hall (Derbyshire), nor has it the pomp of the Jacobean prodigy houses. Montacute rather displays the rich and comfortable final era of Good Queen Bess. This hugely appealed to the Victorians. Montacute was a house much copied during the Jacobethan revival.

The house was built, probably by William Arnold, for a lawyer, Sir Edward Phelips, at the end of the 16th century. Speaker of the House of Commons and Prosecutor of Guy Fawkes, Phelips was also organizer of the spectacular 1612 wedding of James I's only daughter, Princess Elizabeth (later known as the 'Winter Queen'). The same family occupied the house into the 20th century.

In 1915 the house was rented by Lord Curzon, former Viceroy of India and obsessive restorer of English houses (including Bodiam, in Sussex; Tattershall, in Lincolnshire, and his own Kedleston Hall, in Derbyshire). After the death of his first wife, he briefly shared Montacute with his mistress, Elinor

'No house in **Somerset** has a **finer approach,** down a **sweeping avenue ...**'

Glyn, and then (to Glyn's fury) with his second wife. Despite being only a tenant, Curzon spent lavishly on the 'preservation of a lovely thing for the nation'. He stripped the walls of inappropriate paint, rush-matted the floors, rehung the fabrics and filled the house with Tudor furniture.

Following Curzon's death in 1925, the Phelips family decided in 1931 to sell Montacute for scrap. It mercifully escaped this fate under a second benefactor, Ernest Cook, grandson of Thomas. He had made a fortune from the sale of the family travel agency to Wagons Lits, and used the proceeds to buy and give to the National Trust not just Montacute but other properties as well (including Buscot Park, Oxfordshire). The Trust has since struggled to refurnish the house with donated textiles and tapestries, and paintings from the National Portrait Gallery.

No house in Somerset has a finer approach, down a sweeping avenue from the road. The rear façade, however, is not original but a stroke of antiquarian genius of the 1780s. Edward Phelips (the fifth of that name) utilized stonework from an earlier period, from Clifton Maybank near Yeovil, to give himself a new entry to what was the rear of the building. It was this imported façade that so attracted the Victorians. Dating from the mid-16th century, it is of a delicate beauty that contrasts with the rather ponderous Elizabethan towers on either side.

The present visitors' entrance is on the far side, facing the garden. This is a magnificent cliff of Elizabethan architecture. A court of pavilions, walls and strapwork frames the steps rising to the main door. Statues of 'worthies' look down from above. The door leads into the screens passage, with the dining room to the left and the Great Hall to the right. The former was converted in the 18th century from the old buttery and has an eccentric fireplace assembled in the 1780s. It is filled with Tudor portraits. Here hangs a rare surviving masterpiece of French Gothic art, the Tournai *millefleurs* tapestry of 1477, depicting a knight on horseback in a glorious field of flowers.

The Great Hall is not big. By the late 16th century such rooms were losing their communal significance. However, at the far end is a Montacute curio. A frieze shows a man caught drinking when supposedly minding a baby, and being paraded round town tied to a pole as punishment. Why this particular scene, known as the Stang Ride, should adorn the main reception room is a mystery.

Montacute is a big house. The remaining rooms on the ground floor are the parlour and drawing room, much altered but carefully restored. In the drawing room is a hunting portrait by Daniel Gardner and paintings by Reynolds and Gainsborough. Here too is a pair of fierce Chinese 'Dogs of Fo'. The stairs lead to Lord Curzon's bedroom where, in the words of the poem, he presumably 'sinned with Elinor Glyn'. He certainly installed a fine Edwardian bath.

Above There are 42 stained-glass shields set into the library windows at Montacute, some of the most important elements from the original house to have survived. They represent the arms of various branches of the Phelips family and their influential friends and Somerset neighbours. The windows would have looked down on what was then the Great Chamber, where Sir Edward Phelips received his most important guests.

Above The chimney-piece in the dining room is made up of different parts, dating from the Elizabethan era and later, and was put together in the 1780s. **Below** The oak bed in the Crimson Bedroom bears the arms of James I in the centre of the headboard; to the left are the arms of James' son, Henry, Prince of Wales, and to the right, those of his son-in-law, Frederick V, Elector Palatine.

The library was formerly the Great Chamber, a room full of light looking down on the north garden with its yews like guardsmen standing to attention. The room has its original plasterwork frieze and chimneypiece, the latter flanked by classical columns embracing an elaborate heraldic panel. The niches on either side were once filled with nudes, sadly not replaced after their removal by prudish Victorians. The windows carry heraldic glass of the marital activities of the Phelipses. Despite their fine house, from the 17th century to the 20th they lived and died plain Mr.

The Crimson Bedroom has an exquisite frieze but looks strangely naked without its tapestries beneath. Its bed posts are like tree trunks. The second floor is dominated by a Long Gallery, reputedly the longest in England. This has been much altered and displays a set of early portraits from the National Portrait Gallery. The low-light controls entirely wreck the spirit of this gallery, which should be flooded with sun and give views out over the surrounding countryside. Such conservation is a sort of visual vandalism.

Muchelney Abbey was Glastonbury's poorer sister. The Benedictine abbey church has all but vanished, but the abbot's lodgings, which became farmhouses on the Dissolution, are virtually intact and most rare. They include parlours, kitchens and living rooms. At the end of the Middle Ages, a church inspector remarked that the monks lived too well and 'ate in private'. The rooms date from the early years of the 16th century, the last flowering of monastic building.

The lodgings stand tall and bold beyond the displayed footings of the ruined abbey church. They form one side of the old cloister, located at the end of the vanished refectory. To the left of the entrance are two kitchens on either side of a large double fireplace. The steward's range lies beyond. The principal rooms are the downstairs ante-room and the upstairs abbot's parlour, with private closets above the cloister walk. These splendid rooms suggest a lifestyle quite distinct from that of the monks, of whom there were just eleven here at the Dissolution.

The cloister walk is a beautiful relic of the monastery arcade, with high arches and Gothic vaults broken off where a ceiling was inserted. The abbot's parlour is reached up a generous flight of stairs. Its overmantel is decorated with quatrefoils and vine leaves and rises to two carved lions. Pevsner extols this as 'one of the most sumptuous pre-Reformation fireplaces in the country'. The benches are backed by linenfold. Three adjacent rooms, perhaps bedrooms, have their original roofs, one with remains of wall-paintings.

Muchelney abbey

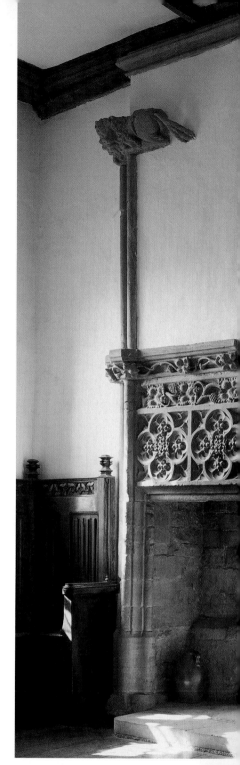

Above and right The fine carved stone fireplace and wooden settle in the Abbot's parlour give some indication of his standing in the community and of the Abbey's wealth. These comfortable lodgings were completed only a few years before the Dissolution of the monasteries in 1539, when the Abbey's lands and property were handed over to the Crown.

Muchelney:
Priest's house

A medieval thatched cottage that remains little changed

At Muchelney, 8 miles NW of Yeovil; National Trust, open part year

This is a chocolate-box cottage. An order to build a priest's house at Muchelney was issued from Wells in 1308. A single span of thatched roof rises above a medieval door with a two-tier hall window to one side. The plan was of the customary hall with upstairs solar at one end and kitchens at the other. The only later alterations were a fireplace and an additional room over the hall. The house was occupied by a priest into the 19th century and was saved from demolition in 1901 by the intervention of Thomas Hardy, Bernard Shaw and William Morris's widow. It is now owned by the National Trust and tenanted.

The house is a gem of medieval architecture. Everything seems original. An old door leads into a screens passage, still of blackened oak. Into this was at some point let a giant slab of Ham stone to support a new fireplace and chimney. This may have been inserted here rather than against an outside wall for extra warmth.

Beyond is the priest's study, with a medieval window and his bedroom above. The main chamber over the hall reveals its old roof beams and part of the hall window rising into its wallspace. Some of the woodwork, including the steep staircase, is not original but the work of Ernest Barnsley of the Cotswold group of architect craftsmen. It is most appropriate.

Nether Stowey: Coleridge cottage

Above The second parlour, or bookroom, of Coleridge cottage would once have been a kitchen. However, it had already been converted by the time Coleridge and his family came to live at Nether Stowey.

✫ A simple cottage that was home to Coleridge when he wrote 'Kubla Khan'

At Nether Stowey, 7 miles W of Bridgwater; National Trust, open part year

No Xanadu this. The picture village of Nether Stowey is placid, just a few houses and the Ancient Mariner pub. Opposite the pub stands the house where Samuel Taylor Coleridge lived for three years with his young wife, Sara, and their son, Hartley. Its appearance is appropriately ascetic.

This is how Coleridge wanted it. The year was 1797 and a publishing venture in London had failed. Coleridge's friend, Thomas Poole, lived in Nether Stowey and Coleridge, close to destitution, insisted on coming down as a neighbour. He wanted no servants, no preaching, one pig and a vegetable garden. He called it his 'dear gutter' and settled down to write poems. He also found 'a large number of very pretty young women in Stowey all musical; I am an immense favourite for I pun, conundrumise, listen and dance'.

The years at Nether Stowey were among Coleridge's most productive. He was visited by his literary friends, including many whose revolutionary attire and demeanour alarmed the locals (and Poole). Here too came the notorious 'person from Porlock', to interrupt the opium-induced reverie of Kubla Khan. The three years at Nether Stowey yielded 'The Rime of the Ancient Mariner', 'Frost at Midnight' and Coleridge's contribution to the Lyrical Ballads.

The cottage would have been thatched at the time, but was reroofed in the 19th century. Only the four front rooms on the ground and upper floors are original. They have been converted into a museum of pictures, manuscripts and memorabilia. This includes a lock of Coleridge's hair, sword and magnificent Boulle ink stand, the latter a particular treasure.

The place is admirably fusty. The custodian, resplendent with a mariner-like white beard, winds up an ancient clock and sells Coleridgiana. It is notoriously hard to bring a writer's house to life. But at least a poet can be read. Here a more vivid touch to Coleridge might perhaps be to have readings from a tape of 'The Ancient Mariner' rather than display one page of an early edition.

Norton St Philip:
The George

⭐ A fine example of a surviving medieval hostelry

At Norton St Philip, 7 miles S of Bath; now a public house and hotel

Here is a rare survivor of medieval hospitality, a true caravanserai. The Carthusian monks of Hinton Priory are said to have established both a lodging house for travellers and a market for their produce. It is today a busy inn with three bars, dining rooms and eight medieval bedrooms to the rear with ancient furniture.

The façade, dominating the centre of the village, is impressive. The ground floor is of stone. The upper floors are black-and-white, jettied and with three idiosyncratic oriel windows. Even more impressive is the rear elevation, three stone storeys surrounding a courtyard. Here the outhouses have Collyweston tiles. An octagonal stair turret leads to a timbered gallery serving the upstairs rooms.

Given the fate of most hotels fashioned from ancient houses, the interiors at the George have fared well. Stalls and partitions are still in place. Fires burn in the grates. The Charterhouse Bar is a medieval hall with beamed ceiling and fireplace. The Monmouth Bar is buried below, with low beams and flagstone floors, named after the rebel commander vanquished at Sedgemoor nearby. It was the last battle fought on English soil, in 1685 (with due respect to various urban 'riots'). The hapless Duke of Monmouth, illegitimate son of Charles II and Protestant pretender to the throne, is said to have rested in this house.

The George is described by Clifton-Taylor as among 'the finest and most venerable of English hostelries'. If ever there was a true 'public house', this is it.

Left The courtyard of the George is home to a pleasing jumble of ancient buildings, reflecting the great age of the inn. There has been a hostelry on this site since the late 13th century when it was built to accommodate merchants visiting the wool fairs that took place in Norton St Philip right up until the beginning of the 20th century.

Porlock: Dovery manor

⭐ Exmoor village manor with spectacular window

At Porlock, 6 miles W of Minehead; museum, open part year

Dovery, or Doverhay, is a medieval house sitting at the head of a picture village beneath a notoriously steep hill leading down from Exmoor. The manor is an L-shaped building comprising entrance hall, solar wing and later addition on the other side. The exterior is most remarkable for its picturesque setting under the slope of the hill, and for the unusually grand hall window facing the street. The interior is splendidly atmospheric.

The window is a square composition, with ogees in the lower tier and curious broken ogees in the upper one. The whole work is beautiful, exuding modest opulence. One would love to know from what pattern book or recollection the local mason who built it derived his inspiration.

The interior was much restored by the Victorians but still has its original room layouts. There is a gigantic fireplace in the hall, as if vying with the window for ostentation, and two further chambers upstairs with plaster ceilings and fireplaces. They are filled with local museum paraphernalia. Like many such places, the whole is more than the sum of its parts.

Stoke-sub-Hamdon: The priory

⭐ Hall house with farm buildings

At Stoke-sub-Hamdon, 6 miles NW of Yeovil; National Trust, open part year

Stoke is for stone. Here 'sub Hamdon' has long been quarried, in my view, the finest limestone in England, the glory of Montacute and houses and churches throughout Somerset and Dorset. It has found a thousand metaphors. Ham is biscuit and honey, liquid gold at dawn and blood red at dusk. Examine it under a magnifying glass and you will find its kaleidoscope reflecting myriad shells and crystals.

How lucky therefore to find the old priory farm still standing in North Street, a chantry foundation of the Provost of Beauchamp. It backs onto the street and fronts onto a yard behind. A porch, screens passage and hall survive and are open to the public. Round it are grouped medieval farm buildings, all in the famous stone.

There is little special to see, just an original hooded doorway and a chapel overlooking the road. The two-storey solar wing also survives. The hall is open to the roof and has a big Tudor window and balcony.

Ston Easton

 An 18th-century mansion built in Queen Anne and Palladian styles

7 miles N of Shepton Mallet; now a hotel

Ston Easton is a grand house of the 1740s yet has no known architect. It was built for the Hippisley family, who acquired the estate at the Dissolution and retained it until 1956. The house was then acquired and restored by the Rees-Moggs before being sold in 1982 and becoming a hotel.

The façade is curious. The central part is of three recessed bays with projecting wings and appears Queen Anne. These wings are then flanked by further wings in a later, Palladian, style. It is all most handsome but a little cold.

The reception rooms are conventionally Georgian, with the exception of the ground-floor saloon. This is said to have been decorated by the younger John Wood of Bath in 1769, although it looks twenty years earlier. A giant roundel carries a relief of Jupiter's eagle in the centre. Pedimented niches at either end contain busts. Panels have *trompe-l'œil* grisailles. Most splendid is the doorway from the hall, a Corinthian composition worthy of a grand London palace.

The dining room, now in bright yellow, displays Chippendale furniture, not all of it original, and family portraits. It is dominated by a painting of house servants in 1770, a poignant tribute to 'below stairs'. The housekeeper in the group is said to have murdered the stillroom maid for kissing the bailiff. Of the other rooms, the library has a classical overmantel framing a picture of the Roman Forum. The house has a rare surviving print room, with 18th-century prints stuck to the walls as decoration.

The park at Ston Easton was laid out, reputedly, by Humphry Repton, and restored by Penelope Hobhouse. It runs down to a stream in a dell below the rear terrace.

Below Classical architecture inspired the plasterwork in the saloon at Ston Easton. Columns and pediments frame the doors and scrolls, shells and other motifs decorate the frieze. At the very centre of the ceiling is a Roman symbol, Jupiter's eagle; an apt choice since the eagle was also the Hippisley family crest.

Tyntesfield

✦ ✦ ✦ A Victorian-Gothic extravaganza with contents intact

At Wraxall, 6 miles SW of Bristol; National Trust, open for guided tours

Unknown Tyntesfield burst onto the map after Lord Wraxall died and left his estate not to his son but to be divided equally between nineteen relatives, Continental fashion. In 2002, the executors concluded that a sale of the entire house and contents was the only option and the National Trust had to gird its loins for battle. It won with Lottery help, and the house was opened to the public in 2003, with admirable dispatch.

The house was re-built from 1863 onwards for the guano tycoon, Anthony Gibbs. A devout Anglo-Catholic, he would walk each day from his London house in Hyde Park to London Docks to inspect the latest shipment of seabird droppings which would be converted into fertilizer. He and his son, William, were to make a phenomenal £100,000 a year in profit. They spent most of it on their house at Tyntesfield, on Keble College, Oxford, and on evangelical churches in the Tractarian cause. At the house they built the largest private-house chapel in England, proclaiming God's glory, a presence amid all this dung and money.

The house emerges from a fold in the Mendip foothills overlooking its own valley. Ramparts of rhododendron and azalea part to offer glimpses of Gothic grey. Turrets, pinnacles and gables loom through trees. Lichen clings to rust-stained windows. The house exterior is of the sort that Thomas Warton described in his lines, 'Lead me, Queen Sublime, to solemn glooms/ Congenial with my soul;/ to cheerless shades,/ To ruin'd seats, to twilight cells and bowers.'

The building was remodelled from an 1813 house by John Norton in 1863, with additions by Henry Woodyer in 1885 and the magnificent chapel by Sir Arthur Blomfield. Its plan is relatively

symmetrical, although not its exterior appearance. This is in the most romantic Gothic style. It survives as built, except for the loss of a once soaring tower over the entrance porch.

The entrance faces the drive, but the main rooms face south over the park. The façades all have Gothic windows, Tudor oriels, chimneys and attic dormers. The building material is grey and even on the sunniest day the effect is severe. This is not true of the interior. Here Norton and Woodyer designed suites of richly ornamented chambers, employing the leading craftsmen of the day. Star was the firm of J. G. Crace, master of Longleat (Wiltshire) and Knightshayes (Devon, see page 101). Tyntesfield retains these interiors intact, including furniture, fabrics and household contents.

Each room is different. The library, filling the wing flanking the courtyard, is open to its roof and is heavy with a splendid Crace-designed carpet. The dining room has a bay devoted to Indian design by Woodyer, its frieze decorated with animals. The staircase hall has a balcony on three sides above bold Gothic arches, overseen by portraits of William Gibbs and his wife,

Matilda. They peopled the hall with busts of Anglo-Catholic divines. The drawing room beyond has a barrel vault, silk wall-hangings and ivory inlaid doors.

Everywhere the craftsmanship is of the first quality. Lord Wraxall's study is decorated with a frieze of fruit and Jacobean scrollwork even on the window shutters. A gigantic moose's head gazes down on the billiard room which has a heated table and electric scoring board. The Tyntesfield estate maps wallpaper a passage. In a rear courtyard are Gothic kennels, as though awaiting the return of their mastiffs.

The house, on my first visit, was a true time warp. It had not been weeded of junk and seemed like a great aristocratic house down on its luck and awaiting bailiffs. Shelves creaked with crockery. Leather books were stacked against walls. Curtains drooped lusciously over furniture. The upstairs rooms were as if guests had just fled in despair, with a telephone receiver hanging from the wall. Everywhere were prints of Gothic churches and religious art. This is a culture not of our time, but I wonder if 'salvation' can really save it.

'Everywhere the craftsmanship is of the first quality.'

Far left Everyday objects that would have played an important part in daily life are placed on display at Tyntesfield; a crowd of walking sticks and a row of hats still await their owners in the entrance hall. **Left** In the main hall, the magnificent balcony and carved stone cantilevered staircase are topped with ornate, gothic-style balusters, unusually made from cast iron. **Below** The billiard room is a sporting shrine, decked with the trophies of long-forgotten hunting trips, including an enormous tiger-skin rug beneath the table.

Wells: Bishop's palace

✩ ✩ An episcopal residence, protected by wall and moat

Market Place, Wells; private house and grounds, open part year

Above Over 150 years ago the daughters of Bishop John Auckland and Bishop Lord Arthur Hervey decided to teach the swans that lived at the Bishop's Palace to ring a bell when they wanted food. Since then, each generation of adult swans has taught the cygnets to pull the bell-rope by the gatehouse window. The very first swan to learn the trick has been preserved and can be seen in nearby Wells Museum.

Above The Bishop of Bath and Wells shares the front lawn of his palace with a croquet club. The club plays on two courts – one half size, one nearly full size – from April to October.
Below It was the first Bishop of Bath and Wells, Jocelin Trotman, who began building the palace in the early 13th century, on land just south of the Cathedral of St Andrew.

There are finer palaces in England but few have settings more picturesque than the home of the Bishop of Bath and Wells. It was intended as a fortress to protect the bishop from the townspeople, an English Albi. It is now a gentle harmony of stone, water and trees.

Even when the precinct is closed, the walk round the moat and the view through its gatehouse are a delight. I once sat on the bank and watched an iridescent kingfisher at work. It darted among the mute swans which are trained to pull a bell rope below a window for their daily feed.

The palace is not what it was. The Great Hall of Bishop Burnell, now a ruin, must have been a gigantic 13th-century chamber. A century later a dispute between Bishop Ralph and the townspeople led to the building of the wall and moat round an enclave covering 13 acres. Had this been left to evolve undisturbed, it would now be a precious medieval survival. Instead it has been gradually cleared and landscaped to form a decorous park, where the Palace Croquet Club meets in summer.

The chapel and ruins of the hall stand to the right of the palace itself. This was drastically altered by the architect, Benjamin Ferrey, in 1846. His ecclesiastical contacts far outstripped his ability. How much he ruined is unclear, for his new façades and interiors are neither Gothick nor robust medieval. The style reflects the 'muscular Christianity' of an English public school.

Inside there is still much worth seeing. The hall is part of the old undercroft, with bold rib-vaulting and a spectacular medieval fireplace. Upstairs, Ferrey designed the Long Gallery and a panelled room, the windows with trefoil or sometimes quinquefoil arches. What appear to be Purbeck marble columns are, in fact, enamelled iron. The wallpaper in the Long Gallery forms a splendid backdrop to a collection of episcopal portraits.

Glossary

The aim in this book has been to avoid terms not familiar to the lay person. However, some specialist terms in common use in architectural circles may have crept in, for which the following definitions may be helpful.

acanthus – pattern of an exotic Mediterranean flower with large leaves used in classical decoration.

anthemion – a honeysuckle flower pattern used in classical decoration.

Artisan Mannerist – buildings created by masons using pattern books (rather than architects) in the period c.1615–75. Mannerism originated in 16th-century Italy and was characterised by Classical elements used in unusual ways. It was taken up in the Low Countries, then spread to England.

ashlar – any block of masonry fashioned into a wall, either load-bearing or covering brick.

bailey, inner and outer – a fortified enclosure, usually moated and surrounded by a curtain wall, containing a motte (mound) on which stands a keep. Walls are topped by battlements, with crenellations which protected defenders from arrows, and machicolations, or floor openings, through which missiles could be fired down on attackers.

baluster – upright post supporting the handrail on stairs.

bargeboard – wooden board protecting the eaves of a roof.

bay – a space of wall between any vertical element, such as an upright beam, pillar or a division into a window or door.

bay window – window projecting out from a flat wall, either canted if the sides are straight, or bowed if curved.

bolection mould – moulding concealing the join of vertical and horizontal surfaces, shaped like an S in cross-section.

Boulle – elaborate inlay work on the surface of furniture, customary in 17th and 18th-century French work.

bow – see bay window

canted – see bay window

cartouche – frame for a picture or statue, often oval and surrounded by a scroll.

caryatid – a column in the shape of a draped female figure.

casements – see sashes

chinoiserie – a style of advanced Rococo with Chinese motifs, often associated with Gothick.

coffering – a ceiling composed of beams enclosing sunken square or round panels.

collars – see roof timbers

corbel – a stone or wood projection in a wall that supports a beam, statue or window sill.

cornice – (1) a ledge or projecting upper part of a classical entablature. (2) Moulding at the top of a wall concealing the join with the ceiling.

cottage ornée – late-Georgian/Victorian picturesque cottage, usually with thatched roof and Gothic windows.

crenellation – see bailey

cruck – a simple structure of two, usually curved, trunks of wood formed into an inverted V which support the walls and roof of a medieval house.

curtain wall – in castle-building, a wall constructed between defensive projections such as bastions.

dressing – a general term for finishings; stone is dressed to either a smooth or ornamental surface.

enfilade – a line of rooms in sequence along one side of a house, usually with interconnecting doors.

entablature – a feature of classical architecture comprising everything above column height, formally composed of architrave, frieze and cornice.

flatwork – decorative plaster or woodwork in low relief.

frontispiece – a decorative bay above a doorway in a Tudor or Jacobean building, customarily composed of Renaissance motifs.

gable – the triangular end of a double-pitched roof, sometimes with stepped or scrolled (Dutch) sides.

garderobe – privy or lavatory, usually discharging into a ditch or moat outside a medieval house.

Great Chamber – see solar

grisaille – monochrome painting, usually a mural and in shades of grey.

grotesque – decorative wall motif of human figures, as found in Roman grottoes.

half-timbering – term for timber-framed house derived from the practice of splitting logs in half to provide beams.

hipped roof – a roof with a sloping end instead of an end gable.

Ho-Ho bird – chinoiserie motif associated with 18th-century Rococo style.

jetty or jettied floor – upper floor extended, or oversailed, beyond the lower one to give more space upstairs and to protect the lower walls from adverse weather. Jettying also uses the downward thrust of the upper walls to form a cantilever, preventing internal ceiling beams from bowing.

keep – see bailey

king post – see roof timbers

linenfold – a pattern on wall panels imitating folded linen.

louvre – a covered turret above a medieval hall that allowed smoke to escape.

machicolation – see bailey

mansard – a roof with two separate pitches of slope.

motte – see bailey

mullion – central divider of window, made of metal or stone.

oversail – see jetty

oriel – an upper window projecting from a wall, sometimes (incorrectly) used to indicate a tall medieval window lighting the dais end of the Great Hall.

Palladian – a style of classical architecture, formal and refined outside, often lavish inside, named after Italian architect, Andrea Palladio (1508–80). Moving spirit behind most English classical designers, especially Inigo Jones and, later, Lord Burlington, William Kent and the early Georgians.

parlour – see solar

piano nobile – the main ceremonial floor of a classical building, sitting on the basement or 'rustic' lower floor.

pier-glass – a wall mirror supported by a small table, bracket or console.

pilaster – a flat column projecting only slightly from a wall.

pointing – mortar or cement used to seal between bricks.

porte-cochère – a grand porch with a driveway through it, allowing passengers to alight from carriages under cover.

prodigy house – a large, ostentatious house of the Elizabethan/Jacobean period.

putti – unwinged sculptures of chubby boys found in Classical and Baroque decoration.

queen post – see roof timbers

quoins – dressed corner stones.

render – a covering of stucco, cement or limewash on the outside of a building.

Rococo – the final phase of Baroque style in the 18th century, typified by refined painted and plaster decoration, often asymmetrical and with figures.

roof timbers – a tie-beam runs horizontally across the roof space; a king post rises vertically from the tie beam to the apex of the roof; queen posts rise not to the apex but to subsidiary beams known as collars; wind-braces strengthen the roof rafters.

rustic – a name given in Palladian architecture to the lower floor or basement, beneath the piano nobile.

rustication – treatment of ashlar by deep-cutting joints so they look stronger or cruder.

sashes – windows opening by rising on sash ropes or cords, as opposed to casements which open on side hinges.

scagliola – composition of artificial stone that imitates appearance of grained marble.

screens passage – accessed from the main door of a medieval building and built into one end of a Great Hall to shield it from draughts. Door ors arches lead from the passage into the hall on one side and kitchens on other. Above is usually a minstrels' gallery.

Serlian – motifs derived from pattern books of the Italian Renaissance architect, Sebastiano Serlio (1475–1554).

sgraffito – plaster decoration scratched to reveal another colour beneath.

solar – the upstairs room at the family end of a medieval hall, originally above an undercroft or parlour. Originally accessed by ladder or spiral stairs, it was usually replaced by a Great Chamber in the Tudor era.

strapwork – strap or ribbon-like decorative scrolls in Elizabethan and Jacobean design.

stucco – plaster, usually protective, covering for brick, sometimes fashioned to look like stone.

studding – vertical timbers laid close to each other to strengthen the wall. Close-studding tends to indicate wealth.

tie-beam – see roof timbers

undercroft – a vaulted room or crypt beneath a building, partly or wholly underground

vault – a ceiling, usually of stone composed of arches.

Venetian window – Palladian window composed of three components, the centre one arched.

wind-braces – see roof timbers

Simon Jenkins' sources

The best guides to any house are the people who occupy it. They have felt its walls and sensed its seasons. They stand witness to its ghosts, real and imagined, and have thus become part of its history. As a substitute, guidebooks vary widely from the academic to the plain childish. The best are published by English Heritage, erudite and enjoyable. National Trust guidebooks are at last moving from the scholarly to the accessible, and the Trust's compendium *Guide*, by Lydia Greeves and Michael Trinick, is excellent.

My selection of a thousand properties derives from numerous sources. These include Hudson's *Historic Houses and Gardens*, supplemented by *Museums and Galleries* published by Tomorrow's Guides. The Historic Houses Association website is another invaluable source. Of recent house surveys, the best are John Julius Norwich's *Architecture of Southern England* (1985), John Martin Robinson's *Architecture of Northern England* (1986) and Hugh Montgomery-Massingberd's *Great Houses of England and Wales* (2000). Nigel Nicolson's *Great Houses of Britain* (1978) describes the most prominent. Their lists are not exhaustive and include houses not open to the public. Behind them stands Nikolaus Pevsner's massive 'Buildings of England' series, which deals with houses more generously (with plans) in the newer revised editions.

On English domestic architecture, the classics are hard to beat. They include Olive Cook's *The English House Through Seven Centuries* (1968), Alec Clifton-Taylor's *The Pattern of English Building* (1972), Hugh Braun's *Old English Houses* (1962), Sacheverell Sitwell's *British Architects and Craftsmen* (1964) and Plantagenet Somerset Fry's *Castles of Britain and Ireland* (1980).

On specific periods the best are Mark Girouard's *Robert Smythson and the English Country House* (1983), Giles Worsley's *Classical Architecture in England* (1995), Kerry Downes's *English Baroque Architecture* (1966) and Girouard's *The Victorian Country House* (1971). Joe Mordaunt Crook takes a lively look at the Victorian battle of the styles in *The Dilemma of Style* (1989). Jeremy Musson describes the manorial revival in *The English Manor House* (1999) and Gavin Stamp takes a wider look at the same period in *The English House 1860–1914* (1986). *Edwardian Architecture*, edited by Alastair Service (1975), brings the story into the 20th century and Clive Aslet's *The Last Country Houses* (1982) almost completes it.

On social history, Girouard's *Life in the English Country House* (1978) is incomparable. *Creating Paradise* (2000) by Richard Wilson and Alan Mackley sets the house in its economic context. So does Mordaunt Crook's *The Rise of the Nouveaux Riches* (1999) and David Cannadine's *The Decline and Fall of the British Aristocracy* (1990). Adrian Tinniswood offers a fascinating insight in his *History of Country House Visiting* (1989). The desperate post-war bid to save houses is described in Marcus Binney's *Our Vanishing Heritage* (1984) and John Cornforth's *The Country Houses of England 1948–1998* (1998). Peter Mandler covers the same period in his scholarly *The Fall and Rise of the Stately Home* (1997).

Biographies of architects are too legion to list but Howard Colvin's *Biographical Dictionary of British Architects* (1978) was my bible over disputed dates and attributions. Of a more personal character is James Lees-Milne's delightful account of the National Trust's early acquisitions in *People and Places* (1992). Houses in distress are visited in John Harris's *No Voice from the Hall* (1998). *Writers and their Houses* (1993) is a first-class collection of essays, edited by Kate Marsh.

I am indebted to the many architectural commentaries in *Country Life*, champion of the historic buildings cause for over a century. I do not believe I could have found a thousand houses for my list were it not for its progenitors, Edward Hudson and Christopher Hussey, and their many successors.

Contact details

Note: Readers are advised to check opening times before visiting, either via the websites and addresses below or in Hudson's *Historic Houses & Gardens*, the annual guide to castles, houses and heritage sites open to the public.

A la Ronde – Summer Lane, Exmouth, Devon, EX8 5BD www.nationaltrust.org.uk/main/placestovisit Tel 01395 265514 Open Apr–Oct, 11am–5.30pm (closed Fri & Sat)

Antony House – Torpoint, Cornwall, PL11 2QA www.nationaltrust.org.uk/main/placestovisit Tel 01752 812191 Open Apr–Oct, Tue–Thur, plus Sun in Jun, Jul & Aug, and Bank Holidays

Arlington Court – Arlington, Nr Barnstaple, Devon, EX31 4LP www.nationaltrust.org.uk/main/placestovisit Tel 01271 850296 House open Apr–Nov (closed Tue), 10.30am–5.30pm; grounds open all year

Barrington Court – Barrington, Ilminster, Somerset, TA19 0NQ www.nationaltrust.org.uk/main/placestovisit Tel 01460 241938 House & gardens open Mar–Oct, from 11am (closed Wed)

Barrington: Strode House – As for Barrington Court. Apartment available for holiday lets all year

Bath: 1 Royal Crescent – 1 Royal Crescent, Bath, BA21 2LR www.bath-preservation-trust.org.uk Tel 01225 428126 Open Feb–Nov (closed Mon except Bank Holidays)

Bath: 16 Royal Crescent – The Royal Crescent Hotel, 16 Royal Crescent, Bath, BA1 2LS www.royalcrescent.co.uk Tel 01225 823333

Bath: Crowe Hall – Widcombe Hill, Bath, BA2 6AR Tel 01225 310322 House open by appointment; gardens open a few afternoons a year, or by appointment

Bath: Herschel House – The William Herschel Museum, 19 New King Street, Bath, BA1 2BL www.bath-preservation-trust.org.uk Tel 01225 311342/446865 Open mid-Jan–mid-Dec (closed Wed)

Bath: Prior Park – Ralph Allen Drive, Bath, BA2 6BD www.nationaltrust.org.uk/main/placestovisit Tel 01225 833422 Gardens open all year (closed Tue and Christmas). (Prior Park House is a school)

Beckford's Tower – Lansdown Rd, Bath, BA1 9BH www.bath-preservation-trust.org.uk Tel 01255 460705 Open Easter–end Oct, Sun, Sat & BH Mon

Beckington: Old Manse – Bath Road, Beckington, Somerset, BA11 6SW Tel 01373 830806 Open by appointment only

Berry Pomeroy Castle – Totnes, Devon, TQ9 6NJ www.english-heritage.org.uk/berrypomeroy Tel 01803 866618 Open daily, Apr–Oct

Bickleigh Castle – Tiverton, Devon, EX16 8RP www.bickleighcastle.com Tel 01884 855363 Open Easter–end Sept, Wed & Sun pm, and by arrangement. Available for weddings, conferences & B&B

Boconnoc House – Estate Office, Boconnoc, Lostwithiel, Cornwall, PL22 0RG www.boconnocenterprises.co.uk Tel 01208 872507 Open by arrangement, plus 4 garden open days for charity; available for weddings and functions

Bodmin Gaol – Berrycombe Road, Bodmin, Cornwall, PL31 2NR Tel 01208 76292 Open daily from 10am

Bristol: Blaise House – Blaise Castle House Museum, Henbury Road, Henbury, Bristol, BS10 7QS www.bristol-city.gov.uk Tel 0117 903 9818 Open all year, Sat–Wed, 10am–5pm

Bristol: The Georgian House – 7 Great George St, Bristol, BS1 5RR www.bristol-city.gov.uk Tel 0117 921 1362 Open all year, Sat–Wed, 10–5pm

Bristol: Kings Weston House – Kings Weston Lane, Kings Weston, Bristol, BS11 0UR www.kingswestonhouse.co.uk Tel 0117 938 2299 Private conference centre, can be booked for weddings, functions etc.

Bristol: Red Lodge – Park Row, Bristol, BS1 5LJ www.bristol-city.gov.uk Tel 0117 921 1360 Open all year, Sat–Wed, 10am–5pm

Broadclyst: Marker's Cottage – Broadclyst, Exeter, Devon, EX5 3HR www.nationaltrust.org.uk/main/placestovisit Tel 01392 461546 Open Mar–Oct, Sun–Tue, 2–5pm

Broomham Farm – King's Nympton, Devon, EX37 9TS Tel 01796 572322 View by arrangement only

Buckland Abbey – Yelverton, Devon, PL20 6EY www.nationaltrust.org.uk/main/placestovisit Tel 01822 853607 Open Mar–Oct (not Thur) and most weekend afternoons for rest of year (not Jan)

Burgh Island Hotel – Burgh Island, Bigbury-on-Sea, Devon, TQ7 4BG www.burghisland.com Tel 01548 810514

Cadhay – Ottery St Mary, Devon, EX11 1QT www.cadhay.org.uk Tel 01404 812999 Open Fri afternoons Jul–Sep, plus some Bank Holiday Mons; available for weddings and functions

Caerhays Castle – Caerhays, Gorran, St Austell, Cornwall, PL26 6LY www.caerhays.co.uk Tel 01872 501310 House open mid Mar–end May, Mon–Fri pm (booking recommended); gardens open daily mid-Feb–end May

Castle Drogo – Drewsteignton, Exeter, Devon, EX6 6PB www.nationaltrust.org.uk/main/placestovisit Tel 01647 433306 House open Mar–Nov (closed Tues), gardens open daily all year

Claverton Manor – The American Museum & Gardens, Claverton Manor, Bath, BA2 7BD www.americanmuseum.org Tel 01225 460503 Open Tue–Sun, 12.00–5.30 Mar–Oct, plus 19 Nov–14 Dec, 2–5.30

Cleeve Abbey – Washford, Nr Watchet, Somerset, TA23 0PS www.english-heritage.org.uk/cleeve Tel 01984 640377 Open daily, Mar–Oct

Clevedon Court – Tickenham Road, Clevedon, Somerset, BS21 6QU www.nationaltrust.org.uk/main/placestovisit Tel 01275 872257 Open end Mar–end Sep on Wed, Thur, Sun & Bank Holiday Mon, 2–5pm

Clovelly: Fisherman's Cottage – Clovelly, Devon www.clovelly.co.uk (Clovelly Village Visitor Centre) Tel 01237 431781 (Visitor Centre) or 01237 431213 (Kingsley museum and shop, opposite Fisherman's Cottage) Clovelly estate and museum open all year

Chysauster Ancient Village – Nr New Mill, Penzance, Cornwall, TR20 8XA www.english-heritage.org.uk/chysauster Tel 07831 757934 Open daily, Mar–Oct

Coleton Fishacre – Brownstone Road, Kingswear, Dartmouth, Devon, TQ6 0EQ www.nationaltrust.org.uk/main/placestovisit Tel 01803 752466 Open Mar–Oct, Wed–Sun

Combe House – Gittisham, Nr Honiton, Devon, EX14 3AD www.thishotel.com Tel 01404 540400

Compton Castle – Marldon, Paignton, Devon, TQ3 1TA www.nationaltrust.org.uk/main/placestovisit Tel 01803 875740 Open Apr–Oct, Mon, Wed, Thur

Cotehele – St Dominick, Saltash, Cornwall, PL12 6TA www.nationaltrust.org.uk/main/placestovisit Tel 01597 351346 House open daily (except Fri) Mar–Oct, garden open all year

Cothay Manor – Greenham, Wellington, Somerset, TA21 0JR Tel 01823 672283 Garden open May–Sep, Wed, Thur, Sun & Bank Holidays; house open to groups by arrangement

Cricket House – Cricket St Thomas Historic Hotel, Chard, Somerset, TA20 4DD www.warnerholidaysonline.co.uk or www.cstwp.co.uk (for wildlife park) Tel 01460 30111

Cullacott – Werrington, Launceston, Cornwall, PL15 8NH www.cullacottholidays.co.uk Tel 01566 772631 Available as holiday lets or view by arrangement

Dartington Hall – Dartington, Totnes, Devon, TQ9 6EL www.dartingtonhall.org.uk Tel 01803 847000 Exterior is accessible to view all year; interior viewing by arrangement

Dartington: High Cross House – As Dartington Hall Tel 01803 864114 Open May–Oct, Tue–Fri, 2–4.30pm

Dillington House – Ilminster, Somerset, TA19 9DT www.dillington.co.uk Tel 01460 52427 Residential educational centre; view by arrangement

Dodington Hall – Nr Nether Stowey, Bridgwater, Somerset, TA5 1LF Tel 01278 741400 (or 01278 732251) Open on 10 days in early summer

Dunster Castle – Dunster, Nr Minehead, Somerset, TA24 6SL www.nationaltrust.org.uk/main/placestovisit Tel 01643 821314 Castle open Mar–Nov from 11.00 am (not Thur & Fri); grounds open daily all year

Endsleigh House – Milton Abbot, Tavistock, Devon, PL19 0PQ Fishing club URL is www.endsleigh-fishing-club.com Tel 01822 870248 Gardens open Apr–Sep, 11am–5pm; by appointment Tue, Wed & Thur

Fairfield – Stogursey, Bridgwater, Somerset, TA5 1PU Tel 01278 732251 Normally open 3 days a week in early summer. Groups by arrangement at other times

Fursdon House – Cadbury, Exeter, Devon, EX5 5JS www.fursdon.co.uk Tel 01392 860860 House and garden open Bank Holiday weeks, Mar–Aug

Gatcombe Court – Flax Bourton, Somerset, BS48 3QT Tel 01275 393141 Open for groups by appointment, May–July

Gaulden Manor – Tolland, Lydeard St Lawrence, Taunton, Somerset, TA4 3PN Tel 01984 667213 House open Jun–Aug for groups by written appointment; gardens open Jun–Aug, 2–5pm on Thur, Sun & Bank Holidays

Glastonbury: Abbot's Kitchen – Glastonbury Abbey, Abbey Gatehouse, Magdalene St, Glastonbury, Somerset BA6 9EL www.glastonburyabbey.com Tel 01458 832267 Open daily, all year

Godolphin House – Godolphin Cross, Helston, Cornwall, TR13 9RE www.godolphinhouse.com Tel 01736 763194 Open Easter–end Sept, and to groups by arrangement all year

Haldon Belvedere – Higher Ashton, Nr Dunchideock, Exeter, Devon, EX6 7QY www.haldonbelvedere.co.uk Tel 01392 833668 Open part yr

Hartland Abbey – Hartland, Bideford, Devon, EX39 6DT www.hartlandabbey.com Tel 01237 441264/441234 or 01884 860225 Open Feb–Oct, 1.30–5.30pm, Sun & Bank Holidays

Hestercombe House – Cheddon Fitzpane, Taunton, Somerset, TA2 8LQ www.hestercombehouse.co.uk Tel 0845 345 9188 House open by arrangement (for functions etc). **Gardens** – www.hestercombegardens.com Tel 01823 413923 Open daily all year

Killerton House – Broadclyst, Exeter, Devon, EX5 3LE www.nationaltrust. org.uk/main/placestovisit Tel 01392 881345 House open mid Mar–end Oct and part Dec, sometimes closed Mon & Tue; park & garden open all eyar

Kingston House – The Kingston Estate, Staverton, Totnes, Devon, TQ6 6AR www.kingston-estate.co.uk Tel 01803 762235

Kitley House Hotel – Yealmpton, Nr Plymouth, Devon, PL8 2NW www.kitleyhousehotel.com Tel 01752 881555

Knightshayes Court – Bolham, Tiverton, Devon, EX16 7RQ www.nationaltrust.org.uk/main/placestovisit Tel 01884 254665 House & garden open Mar–Oct, daily from 11.00 (house closed Fri)

Lanhydrock – Bodmin, Cornwall, PL30 5AD www.nationaltrust.org.uk Tel 01208 265950 House open Mar–Oct, daily from 11.00 (closed Mon); garden open all year, daily from 10.00

Launceston Castle – Castle Lodge, Launceston, Cornwall, PL15 7DR www.english-heritage.org.uk/launceston Tel 01566 772365 Open Mar–Oct, daily from 10.00

Lytes Cary Manor – Nr Charlton Mackrell, Somerset, TA11 7HU www.nationaltrust.org.uk/main/placestovisit Tel 01458 224471 Open Mar–Oct, 11am–5pm (closed Mon, Tue, Thur)

Martock: Treasurer's House – Martock, Somerset, TA12 6JL www.nationaltrust.org.uk/main/placestovisit Tel 01935 825801 Open Mar–Sep, 2–5pm, on Sun, Mon & Tue

Montacute House – Montacute, Somerset, TA15 6XP www.nationaltrust.org.uk/main/placestovisit Tel 01935 823289 House open Mar–Oct, 11am–5pm (closed Tue); gardens open all year, 11am–6pm (closed Tue; in winter also closed Mon and close at 4pm)

Mount Edgcumbe – Cremyll, Torpoint, Cornwall, PL10 1HZ www.mountedgcumbe.gov.uk Tel 01752 822236 Open end Mar–Sep, 11am–4.30pm, Sun–Thur

Muchelney Abbey – Muchelney, Langport, Somerset, TA10 0DQ www.english-heritage.org.uk/muchelney Tel 01458 250664 Open daily, end Mar–Oct, from 10am

Muchelney: Priest's House – Muchelney, Langport, Somerset, TA10 0DQ www.nationaltrust.org.uk/main/placestovisit Tel 01458 253771 Open end Mar–Sep, 2–6pm, Sun & Mon

Nether Stowey: Coleridge Cottage – 35 Lime Street, Nether Stowey, Bridgwater, Somerset, TA5 1NQ Tel 01278 732662 www.nationaltrust. org.uk/main/placestovisit Open Apr–Sep, 2–5pm, Thur–Sun

Newton Abbot: Bradley – Newton Abbot, Devon, TQ12 6BN www.nationaltrust.org.uk/main/placestovisit Tel 01626 354513 Open Apr–Sep, 2–5pm, Tue, Wed & Thur

Norton St Philip: The George – The George Inn, Norton St Philip, Bath, Somerset, BA2 7LH www.thegeorgeinn-nsp.co.uk Tel 01373 834224

Paignton: Oldway Mansion – Paignton, Devon, TK www.torquay.com Tel 01803 201201 Open all year, although some rooms may be closed

Pencarrow – Bodmin, Cornwall, PL30 3AG www.pencarrow.co.uk Tel 01208 841369 Open Mar–Oct, 11am–5pm, Sun–Thur

Pendennis Castle – Falmouth, Cornwall, TR11 4LP www.english-heritage.org.uk/pendennis Tel 01326 316594 Open daily all year (times vary); closed Christmas and New Year Bank Holidays

Plymouth: The Elizabethan house – 32 New St, Plymouth, Devon, PL8 7FW Tel 01752 304774 Museum open May–Sep, 10am–5pm, Tue–Sat and Bank Holidays

Plymouth: The Merchant's House – 33 St Andrew's Street, Plymouth, Devon, post code TK Tel 01752 304774 Museum open May–Sep, 10am–5pm, Tue–Sat and Bank Holidays (closed lunchtime, 1–2pm)

Plymouth: The Prysten House – Finewell Street, Plymouth, Devon, PL1 2AD Tel 01752 661414 Open Apr–Sep, 10am–4pm, Mon–Sat

Poltimore House – Friends of Poltimore House, PO Box 409, Exeter, Devon, EX4 5WZ www.poltimore.org

Porlock: Dovery Manor – Doverhay, Porlock, Minehead, Somerset, TA24 8PS Tel 01643 862316 Open May–Sep, 10am–5pm, Mon–Sat (closed for lunch and at 4.30 Sat)

Powderham Castle – Kenton, Exeter, Devon, EX6 8JQ www.powderham. co.uk Tel 01626 890243 Open Mar–Oct, 10am–5.30pm (closed Sat)

Prideaux Place – Padstow, Cornwall, PL28 8RP www.prideauxplace.co.uk Tel 01841 532411 Open Easter and May–Oct (closed Fri & Sat)

Puslinch – Yealmpton, Plymouth, Devon, PL8 2NN Tel 01752 880555 Open for groups by arrangement only

Restormel Castle – Lostwithiel, Cornwall, PL22 0BD www.english-heritage.org.uk/restormel Tel 01208 872687 Open Mar–Oct, daily from 10am

St Mawes Castle – St Mawes, Cornwall, TR2 3AA www.english-heritage.org.uk/stmawes Tel 01326 270526 Open all year, daily from 10am (closed Tue, Wed & Thur in winter and at Christmas and New Year)

St Michael's Mount – Marazion, Nr Penzance, Cornwall, TR17 0EF www.nationaltrust.org.uk or www.stmichaelsmount.co.uk Tel 01736 710507 (710265 for tide info) Open Mar–Oct, daily 10.30–5.30 (closed Sat); open in winter when tide and weather conditions are favourable

Saltram House – Plympton, Plymouth, Devon, PL7 1JH www.nationaltrust. org.uk/main/placestovisit Tel 01752 333500 House open Mar–Oct, 12–4.30 (11.30–3.30 in Oct), daily except Fri; garden open all year from 11am (weekends only in Jan, and closed Thur & Fri in Feb)

Sand – Sidbury, Sidmouth, EX10 0QN www.eastdevon.net/sand Tel 01395 597230 House open on selected days and by arrangement; gardens open 3 days a week, Apr–Sep

Shute Barton – Shute, Axminster, Devon EX3 7PT www.nationaltrust.org.uk/ main/placestovisit Tel 01297 34692 Open Apr–Oct, 2–5.30pm, Wed & Sat

Sidmouth: Sidholme – Sidholme Hotel, Elysian Fields, Vicarage Road, Sidmouth, EX10 8UJ Tel 01395 513633

Stoke-sub-Hamdon: The Priory – North St, Stoke-sub-Hamdon, Somerset, TA4 6QP www.nationaltrust.org.uk/main/placestovisit Tel 01985 843600 Open Mar–Oct, daily 10am–6pm

Ston Easton – Ston Easton Hotel, Ston Easton, Nr Bath, Somerset, BA3 4DF www.stoneaston.co.uk Tel 01761 241631

Tapeley Park – Instow, Bideford, Devon, EX39 4NT Tel 01271 342558 Open Mar–Oct, 10am–5.30pm (closed Sat)

Tintagel Old Post Office – Tintagel, Cornwall, PL34 0DB www.nationaltrust.org.uk CK Tel 01840 770024 Open daily Mar–Oct, 11am–5.30pm (closes at 4pm in Oct)

Tiverton Castle – Tiverton, Devon, EX16 6RP www.tivertoncastle.com Tel 01884 253200/255200 Open Easter–end Oct, 2.30–5.30pm, on Sun, Thur & Bank Holiday Mons, and to groups of 12 or more at any time by appointment

Trerice – Kestle Mill, Nr Newquay, Cornwall, TR8 4PG www.nationaltrust. org.uk/main/placestovisit Tel 01637 875404 Open Mar–Oct, 11am–5.30pm (5pm in Oct); daily except Sat (closed also Tue except in Aug)

Trewithen – Grampound Road, Truro, Cornwall, TR2 4DD www.trewithen-gardens.co.uk Tel 01726 883647 House open Apr–Jul, 2-4pm, Mon & Tue, plus Aug Bank Holiday Mon; gardens open Feb–Sep, 10am–4.30pm, Mon–Sat, plus Sun in Mar, Apr & May

Tyntesfield – Wraxall, Somerset, BS48 1NT www.nationaltrust.org.uk/ tyntesfield Tel 0870 458 4500 Open Sep–Oct, Wed, Sat & Sun, house 11am–4pm, garden 10–5.30pm

Wells: Bishop's Palace – Market Place, Wells, Somerset, BA5 2PD www.bishopspalacewells.co.uk Tel 01749 678691 Open Mar–Oct, 10.30am–6pm Mon–Fri, 12–6pm Sun (closed Sat)

Ugbrooke House – Chudleigh, Devon, TQ13 0AD www.ugbrooke.co.uk Tel 01626 852179 Open Jul–Sep, 1–5.30pm, on Sun, Tue, Wed & Thur, and at other times in Apr–Sep to groups of more than 20 by arrangement

Index

Main entries for houses are in **bold**

T=top TL=top left TR=top right B=bottom BL=bottom left BR=bottom right
L=left R=right C=centre CL=centre left CR=centre right

Front Cover The National Trust/John Hammond (main stairs at Castle Drogo)
Back Cover The National Trust/David Garner (A la Ronde) **Endpapers** The National Trust/John Hammond (Elizabethan 'black work' pillowcase, Antony House) **1** Fursdon House (carving in entrance hall) **2-3** The National Trust/Andrew Besley (gatehouse at Lanhydrock) **4-7** European Map Graphics Ltd. **8** Quintin Wright **10-13** © Reader's Digest/Illustrations by Hardlines Ltd **14-15** www.lastrefuge.co.uk/Dae Sasitorn **16 T** The National Trust/Stephen Robson **B** The National Trust/Mark Bolton **17-18** The National Trust/Andreas von Einsiedel **19** Boconnoc Estate **20** Hugh Price **21** Collections/Paul Watts **22** © Twinkle Treffry / Caerhays Collection **22-23** Collections/Paul Watts **24** www.lastrefuge.co.uk/Dae Sasitorn **25** English Heritage/Max Alexander **26-27 T** The National Trust/Andrea Jones **B** The National Trust/Andreas von Einsiedel **27-28** The National Trust/Andreas von Einsiedel **29 TL** Mary Cole **R** John Davey **30 TL** courtesy of Godolphin House, Helston/photo Paul Raeside **R** Collections/Michael Jenner **31** courtesy of Godolphin House, Helston/photo Paul Raeside **32-33** Collections/Paul Watts **34-37** The National Trust/Andreas von Einsiedel **37 TR** Collections/Quintin Wright **BL** The National Trust/Andreas von Einsiedel **38** Collections/Roy Westlake **39** Mount Edgcumbe House. **40** Collections/Paul Watts **41** Courtesy of the Molesworth-St.Aubyn family **42** English Heritage/Mike Hesketh-Roberts **42-43** Collections/Michael Jenner **43 TL** www.bridgeman.co.uk/Private Collection **44-45** Collections/Paul Watts **46** Prideaux Place **47** www.lastrefuge.co.uk/Dae Sasitorn **48** English Heritage/Andrew Tryner **49** Rupert Tennison **50-51** The National Trust/David Noton **52** Rupert Tennison **53** The National Trust/Andreas von Einsiedel **54** The National Trust/Derek Croucher **54-55** The National Trust/John Bethell **56-59** John Parker **60-62** The National Trust/David Garner **63** The National Trust/Matthew Antrobus **64** The National Trust/Andreas von Einsiedel **64-65** The National Trust/Nadia MacKenzie **66** English Heritage/Jonathan Bailey **67 T** Bickleigh Castle **B** rogerstatenphotography **68** The National Trust/Chris King **69** rogerstatenphotography **70 L** The National Trust/Derek Croucher **70-71** The National Trust/George Wright **71 TR** The National Trust/George Wright **B** www.bridgeman.co.uk/Kunsthistorisches Museum, Vienna, Austria **72** The National Trust/George Wright **73** Neil Holden **74 BL** Popperfoto **74-75** David Lyons **75** Neil Holden **76-77** Collections/Quintin Wright **78-79** www.lastrefuge.co.uk/Dae Sasitorn **79-81** The National Trust/James Mortimer **82** rogerstatenphotography **83** The National Trust/Stephen Robson **84** Combe House **85** The National Trust/Ian Shaw **86-88** John Parker **89** By Permission of the Dartington Hall Trust/© Sam Bailey **90** © Hotel Endsleigh **91** Fursdon House **92** Devon Historic Buildings Trust **93** Hartland Abbey **94** Collections/Quintin Wright **95** Hartland Abbey **96** The National Trust/Dennis Gilbert **97** The National Trust/Andrew Butler **98-99** John Parker **100** Kitley House Hotel **101** John Parker **102-103** The National Trust/Andreas von Einsiedel **104-105** John Parker **106 L** John Parker **R** Reproduced by kind permission of Torbay Library Services **106-107** www.flairphotos.co.uk **108** Plymouth City Museums & Art Gallery Collection **108-110** John Parker **110 B** Collections/McQuillan & Brown **111 T** rogerstatenphotography **B** © Friends of Poltimore House (photo Rikki Apps) **112-114** Courtesy of Powderham Castle and the Earl and Countess of Devon **115** rogerstatenphotography **116** The National Trust/Rupert Truman **117-119** The National Trust/Andreas von Einsiedel **120** © Grains of Sand **121** The National Trust/Ian Shaw **122** Courtesy of Christian Guild Holidays **123** Andrew Lawson **124** Tiverton Castle **124-125** Reproduced with permission of Lord and Lady Clifford **126-127** The National Trust/David Noton **128** The National Trust/Nadia Mackenzie **129** www.lastrefuge.co.uk/Dae Sasitorn **130** The National Trust/Derek Croucher **131** Collections/Quintin Wright **132-133** Collections/Simon McBride **133** The Royal Crescent Hotel. **134 L** www.bridgeman.co.uk/© Victoria Art Gallery, Bath and North East Somerset Council **R** www.bridgeman.co.uk/Private Collection **135 TL** Max Whitaker/Herschel Museum **TR** John Parker **BL** Max Whitaker/Herschel Museum **136** John Parker **137** The National Trust/Joe Cornish **138-139** © Beckford Tower Trust **139** John Parker **140-141** Photo by Neill Menneer **142-143** Courtesy of Kings Weston House **144 T** Max Whitaker **B** Collections/Quintin Wright **145** Reproduced by permission of the American Museum in Britain, Bath **146** English Heritage/© Skyscan Balloon Photography **147** English Heritage/Jonathan Bailey **148 TL** The National Trust/John Blake **148-149** The National Trust/Andreas von Einsiedel **150 TL** Collections/Quintin Wright **150-151** The Interior Archive/Christopher Simon Sykes **152** Country Life/Clive Boursnell **153** The Interior Archive/Christopher Simon Sykes **155** Courtesy of Dillington House **156** Courtesy of Lady Gass **157** The National Trust/Magnus Rew **158 L** The National Trust/Bill Batten **R** The National Trust/John Hammond **159** The National Trust/Nadia Mackenzie **160** Courtesy of Lady Gass **161** Gatcombe Court **162-163** rogerstatenphotography **164** Collections/Philip Craven **165** Skyscan/B. Lea **166** Collections/Robin Williams **167** The National Trust/Stephen Robson **168** The National Trust/Nadia Mackenzie **169** John Parker **170-171** The National Trust/Derek Croucher **172-173** The National Trust/Rupert Truman **173 B** The National Trust **174 BL** English Heritage/Mike Hesketh-Roberts **174-175** English Heritage/Paul Highnam **175** John Parker **176** The National Trust **177** John Parker **178** Graham Haw **178-179** The National Trust/Alan North **179-180** www.vonessenmedia.co.uk **181** The National Trust/Andrew Butler **182 L** The National Trust/Nadia Mackenzie **R** The National Trust/Andreas von Einsiedel **183** The National Trust/Andreas von Einsiedel **184-185** Michael Blandford

Discover Britain's Historic Houses: West Country

Reader's Digest Project Team
Series editor Christine Noble
Art editor Jane McKenna
Picture researcher Christine Hinze
Writer Caroline Smith
Proofreader Ron Pankhurst
Indexer Marie Lorimer
Production Controller Katherine Bunn

Reader's Digest General Books
Editorial director Julian Browne
Art director Nick Clark
Managing editor Alastair Holmes
Picture resource manager Martin Smith
Pre-press account manager Penelope Grose

Colour origination Colour Systems Limited, London
Printed and bound in Europe by Arvato, Iberia

We are committed to both the quality of our products and the service we provide to our customers. We value your comments, so please feel free to contact us on **08705 113366** or via our web site at **www.readersdigest.co.uk**

If you have any comments or suggestions about the content of our books, you can contact us at: **gbeditorial@readersdigest.co.uk**

Published by The Reader's Digest Association Limited, 11 Westferry Circus, Canary Wharf, London E14 4HE

© The Reader's Digest Association Limited 2005

www.readersdigest.co.uk

® Reader's Digest, The Digest and the Pegasus logo are registered trademarks of the Reader's Digest Association, Inc., of Pleasantville, New York, USA.

This book was designed, edited and produced by The Reader's Digest Association Limited based on material from *England's Thousand Best Houses* by Simon Jenkins, first published by Allen Lane, the Penguin Press, a publishing division of Penguin Books Ltd.

Copyright © Simon Jenkins 2003

Concept code   UK0149/L/S
Book code   634-002-01
ISBN   0 276 44067 6
Oracle code   356600002H.00.24